LINDA GEORGIAN

Your Guardian

ANGELS

Use the Power of Angelic Messengers
to Enrich and Empower Your Life

F

A FIRESIDE BOOK • Published by Simon & Schuster
New York London Toronto Sydney Tokyo Singapore

FIRESIDE
Rockefeller Center
1230 Avenue of the Americas
New York, New York 10020

Designed by Pei Loi Koay
Manufactured in the United States of America

1   3   5   7   9   10   8   6   4   2

Library of Congress Cataloging-in-Publication Data
Georgian, Linda M.
Your guardian angels : use the power of angelic messengers to enrich and empower your life /
Linda Georgian
p. cm.
1. Guardian angels. 2. Guides (Spiritualism)
I. Title.
BT966.2.G46   1994
235'.3—dc20   94-17500   CIP

ISBN 0-671-88126-4

The poem "I Never Saw a Moor" on page 31 is reprinted by permission of the publishers and the Trustees of Amherst College from The Poems of Emily Dickinson, *Thomas H. Johnson, ed., Cambridge, Mass.: The Belknap Press of Harvard University Press, copyright 1951, 1955, 1979, 1983 by the President and Fellows of Harvard College.*

Acknowledgments

THIS BOOK HAS BEEN A JOURNEY, and I have not taken it alone. I would like to thank my former personal assistant Darline Beck, for her thirteen years of undying devotion; Sy and Kathy Bonem, for helping me to be at the right place at the right time; another former personal assistant, Casey Brennan, for coming into my life exactly when I needed her; Marge and Irv Cowan, my dear friends who have been such an enormous help to me throughout my life's work; and my friend Nina L. Diamond, a writer and editor who guided this book every step of the way.

Thanks to Erica and Alan, for the use of their extensive personal library of books on Judaism and spirituality; to Lynn Franklin, my tireless agent and loyal friend; to Cassie Jacoby, a fellow angel devotee and truly eternal friend; to Jacqueline Janssen for her vision and faith in me, and for being a human angel who has truly helped me both professionally and personally in every possible way; to Randal Jurkas, my former business and promotional manager, for all his years of hard work and his belief in my spiritual mission; to Bill Lirio, a fellow truth-seeker and friend, who is more like family; to my editor Sydny

Miner, for making this such a delightful experience; to my dear friend Sheila MacRae, who has been so supportive and helpful for many years; to John Nero, who guided me physically, spiritually, and even nutritionally with his devoted friendship; to my sister Sandra Post and my niece Patti Post, who are always there for me; to Debbie Rowley, one of my spiritual colleagues, for sharing with me the experience of meditation and tuning into the angels; and my nephew Daniel Silagy and his family for their love and support.

So many others have given their love, their time, their support, and their knowledge. Thanks to my stepfather, Howard Simmons, for his friendship and love; to author Terry Lynn Taylor, for her informative and inspiring words; to my personal assistant and cheerleader, Wendy Thomas, for her prayers and friendship; to the insightful Mike Warren of Inphomation, Inc., who in the last few years has given me tremendous opportunities; to my kindred spirit and infomercial co-host Dionne Warwick, who shares my spiritual quest; to the late Rev. Jewel Williams, for opening up a whole new spiritual world for me; and to Mindi Rudan, Pam Johnson, Juanita Mazzarella, Laura Caster, Rob Killheffer, and Howard Libin, whose eye-opening conversations were instrumental in the writing of this book.

Special thanks to my beloved mother, Marie Georgian Simmons, who inspired and supported me, who passed along her spiritual, intuitive, and healing abilities, and who now watches over me from spirit; to my loving father, Anthony Georgian, who is now in spirit with my mother and guiding me; to my other loved ones who have passed over and now watch from the spirit world; to my dog, Smarty, who always knows when I need a hug and is always there to give it; and to God, Jesus, and the angels, for their eternal guidance.

TO ALL THOSE PEOPLE who feel alone, who feel they have no mission; to the truth-seekers, and seekers of all kinds; to those who have an abundance of material riches, but who are missing the spiritual riches; to those enduring pain, hardship, and tragedy. May the angels comfort all of you and bring you security so that you, too, may fly with the angels.

Your Guardian ANGELS

Contents

Part One: A JOURNEY WITH THE ANGELS   13

Part Two: ANGEL LORE   33

- The Celestial Hierarchy   46
- The Archangels   49

Part Three: ANGEL AWARENESS   65

- How and Why Do Angels Come to Us?   70
- Under What Circumstances Should We Call upon Them?   78
- What Can They Do for Us?   83
- What Can't They Do for Us?   106
- How Do They Teach Us Lessons?   107
- What About Free Will?   113
- What Are Our Responsibilities?   116
- How Do We Know If a Feeling Is a Message from the Angels?   118
- Are Intuition and Angelic Messages the Same Things?   120
- Do You Have to Believe in or Practice Organized Religion to Believe in Angels or Receive Their Assistance?   124
- How Does Faith Differ from Religious and Cultural Practices, Traditions, and Doctrines?   125

Part Four: Cᴏᴍᴍᴜɴɪᴄᴀᴛɪɴɢ ᴡɪᴛʜ Aɴɢᴇʟs   127

• How Do I Ask for Angelic Assistance?   *129*
• Natural Communication   *131*
• We Don't Always Get What We Want   *133*
• Ignoring Angelic Assistance   *134*
• Will I Actually See an Angel in Body or Light Form?   *140*
• How Quickly Do God's Messengers Answer Us?   *143*
• What Forms Do the Answers Take?   *145*
• What Does It Mean When We Say, "Be Careful What You Ask For, You May Get It," and How Does That Affect Us?   *147*
• What Happens If I Ignore Their Messages?   *148*
• Do the Angels Ever Do Things for Me Without Being Asked?   *153*
• How Do I Know If an Event Is the Result of Angelic Assistance?   *167*

Eᴘɪʟᴏɢᴜᴇ   171

Part One

A JOURNEY WITH THE ANGELS

✳

The reason why birds can fly

and we can't is simply that they

have perfect faith, for to have

faith is to have wings.

—J. M. BARRIE, *THE LITTLE WHITE BIRD*

✳

FRIEND TOLD ME TWO jokes she'd heard recently that illustrate perfectly our quandary about divine assistance: How do we know when events are orchestrated by God? How do we know if the angels, God's messengers, are helping us out? These jokes, she said, make us think: How much do we have to do? Can we just sit back and wait for a miracle? How much exactly is *our part*?

It had been raining all day when a man drove his Jeep over to Mr. Jones's house out in the country to check on the eighty-year-old farmer.

"Mr. Jones!" the man yelled from his Jeep at the old man sitting on the porch. "The rain's gettin' pretty bad and they say the river's risin'. You'd better get out of here. I'll give you a ride. C'mon, hop in!"

"No thanks," Mr. Jones replied. "I'll be just fine. God's gonna take care of me."

"Are you sure, Mr. Jones?" the man asked.

"Yep," Mr. Jones insisted. "You run along now, sonny. God's gonna take care of me."

Well, it rained and it rained and it rained. And by early evening, Mr. Jones's country road was flooding. The water rose so high that Mr. Jones couldn't sit on the porch anymore. He climbed a ladder to the porch roof and sat down.

A neighbor paddled by in a canoe.

"Mr. Jones, the water's gettin' pretty high. Why don't you come with me?" the neighbor suggested.

"No thanks," Mr. Jones replied. "I'll be just fine. God's gonna take care of me."

"Are you sure, Mr. Jones?" the neighbor asked.

"Yep," Mr. Jones insisted. "You paddle along now, sonny. God's gonna take care of me."

The rain continued all night. The water rose so high around Mr. Jones's house that he had to climb onto the roof to stay dry.

Around midnight a sheriff's helicopter flew in and hovered over Mr. Jones's house. Through a loudspeaker, Mr. Jones heard the voice of a sheriff's deputy.

"Mr. Jones, we're here to help you. I'm going to lower this basket and you climb in. Don't worry, you'll be safe," the deputy yelled.

"No thanks," Mr. Jones yelled back up to the helicopter. "You fly along now, sonny. God's gonna take care of me."

"Are you sure, Mr. Jones?" the deputy shouted back.

"Yep," Mr. Jones insisted. "Now, fly off! God's gonna take care of me."

The helicopter flew off into the night.

By 2:00 A.M., Mr. Jones was frantic. The water was so high now that there was hardly a dry spot on the roof. He stood at the highest peak, looked up toward the heavens, raised his hands, and cried out: "God, how could you do this to me! I thought you were gonna *save* me!"

The heavens opened, light poured down on Mr. Jones, and

he heard the clear, booming voice of God: "WHO DO YOU THINK SENT THE JEEP, THE CANOE, AND THE HELICOPTER?!"

Makes you think, doesn't it? How do we recognize divine assistance? Perhaps we think that it only comes with extreme coincidence or larger-than-life miracles? And because of these misconceptions we miss the perfectly normal, even little things that God sends us, or does for us.

The second joke raises more questions.

A man walks into the synagogue to pray on a Saturday morning, just as he's done all his life. But this Saturday is different. He's got a special request. So, after services, when everyone else has gone home, he stays behind, and sitting in the sanctuary, he has a talk with God.

"God," he says. "I need a favor. It's not for me, it's for my family. I need to win the lottery. I know it's a lot to ask, but, like I said, it's not for me. My mother needs an operation, my son needs braces on his teeth, my daughter's in college. I just don't have enough money to take care of all of them. I make a nice living, but I don't have enough. They need my help and I don't know what else I can do. So, God, can you please help me win the lottery?"

The man goes home, and when the lottery winners are announced that week he's heartbroken because he hasn't won. The next Saturday he's back at the synagogue praying.

"God," he says. "Maybe you didn't understand when I was here last week. I need to win the lottery. I'm not a selfish man. This isn't for me. It's for my family. My mother needs an operation, my son needs braces on his teeth, my daughter's in col-

lege, and now I find out that we need new plumbing! I just
don't have enough to take care of all this. *Please*, God, I need
to win the lottery!"

The man goes home again, and when the lottery winners are
announced he's sure he'll win, but he doesn't. He's in tears as
he prays to God in the synagogue the following Saturday.

"God," he cries out. "Can't you hear me praying? I need to
win the lottery. I *swear* it's not for me. It's for my family. I'm a
good man, I work hard, and they need *so* much, and I can't give
it to them. My mother needs an operation, my son needs
braces, my daughter's in college, we need new plumbing, and
now I find out this week that my wife has a thyroid condition.
God, *help* me win the lottery!"

Well, the heavens open, and light beams down into the synagogue sanctuary, as the man hears the unmistakable voice of
God: "SOL, MEET ME HALFWAY . . . BUY A TICKET!!"

We're in a partnership with God, the divine force, the Higher
Power, whatever you're comfortable calling it, him, her.

So, Mr. Jones, you've gotta learn how to *recognize* help when
it's sent. And Sol, you've gotta do *your* part. Metaphorically
speaking, we've all gotta *buy a ticket*.

I always believed in angels, even before I knew what they did.

In church we heard that they flutter around. And my mother
told me that the angels are always here, and that I had one of
my very own, maybe more. I believed her.

One day, while on my tricycle, I got the idea that riding up
the stairs would be a great thing to do. I was only four, so I
didn't know yet that tricycles and stairs don't go together.

As soon as I'd thought of this brilliant plan, I felt the opposite notion in my mind. The little voice said, "Don't do it." But I was four and didn't know yet that you should listen to that little voice because it often knows more than you do. So I bravely and eagerly rode my tricycle up the stairs. Well, I attempted it. Obviously I didn't get very far, and I fell. The tumble knocked a tooth out, but it was only a baby tooth. No harm done, really. It could have been a lot worse.

That's my first recollection of the little voice, the gut feeling . . . my guardian angel. I hadn't followed its suggestion and, tooth in hand, wished I *had*.

Guardian angels and angels in general are a big part of a Catholic upbringing. I learned early on that they do more than flutter around. My mother taught me that our instincts, the little voice we each have inside us, our intuition, is the voice of angels, passing divine assistance from God. She told me that you can always hear it if you just pay attention. And that you can talk back, too, and actually *communicate* with the angels. I was pretty fortunate that she told me that part; most people don't learn that at such an early age. Some people don't learn that *ever*.

My mother was a pretty remarkable woman. She was very conventional in one sense, with her rosary and her candles, but she had her unconventional side, too. All her life she was able to heal people with her hands. She said that the angels worked through them. She never made a big deal about it, but at family gatherings, if someone had an ache or pain, they knew who to come to.

She was also blessed with great intuitive powers and psychic gifts. She said they were a gift from God, messages via angel express. She said that her father (who I never knew because he had already passed on) had these gifts, too. The two of them were the only ones in her family with this kind of ability.

And then I came along.

As I grew older, it became clear that I had the gifts of my mother and grandfather. I grew up with these abilities, this openness, and it felt perfectly natural.

My father believed in God but never discussed religion or spirituality. He kept his thoughts to himself, but he always made sure that I went to church on Sunday.

My older sister, Sandra, fell somewhere in the spectrum between my father and my mother. She had a spiritual sense, but her experiences were quite mild.

By the time I was five years old, I had a personal relationship with my guardian angels. Not only did I know how to be open and trust that inner voice, but I knew how to ask for help, too. That didn't mean that I always followed their guidance! Sometimes kids, even ones who know better, can be pretty stubborn.

Like the day I fell into the creek.

My backyard was a 365-acre golf course. My father was the greenskeeper for the city of Cleveland golf courses, and we lived in a two-story building in the complex that housed the clubhouse and pro shop. Many other families of the era, the late forties and fifties, lived above their places of business, but my father's business wasn't a shoe store or a deli, it was a golf course.

What a great way to grow up! I had what seemed like a forever stretch of green to play in, and trees, and my very own creek. I'd go for long walks and pray, then go looking for little frogs and fish.

One day, when I was ten, I went walking on the golf course, and along the creek. The rocks bordering the water were slippery, and the little voice inside warned me: "Watch out!" But I ignored it and kept going, tiptoeing along the rocks, and oops! Slipped right into the creek.

Divine assistance is pretty handy, but if you ignore it, it doesn't do you much good.

I came out of the creek a little soggy but otherwise okay.

I had a very typical middle-class family. All of my grandparents were from Palermo, Sicily, so growing up in my family was a lot like what you see in the movies—the typical Italian excitement, emotion, and intensity.

My mother, Marie, and my father, Anthony, encouraged us academically, athletically, and socially. The loving environment of our home, which my mother had decorated with a statue here, a cross there, and plenty of religious pictures, gave us the confidence we'd need out in the world.

I loved school and sports, and loved winning awards for both: history, English, French, soccer, field hockey, track and field, softball, golf, and baton twirling. I seemed to have an innate self-discipline and actually *liked* studying, so no one ever had to remind me to do my homework or prepare for a test. I had a perfectionist streak, and what I wanted most was to stay at the top of my class.

If I had a test, I sensed that the angels were helping me. They protected me when I played sports. I grew up feeling blessed. Of course, it helped if I followed what the inner voice said. Whenever I didn't, as on the tricycle and at the creek, I'd end up in a jam.

In times of need, or when I was worried or afraid, I'd think about my guardian angels. It would calm me. The message was: "We're taking care of things, so don't worry."

Then, extraordinary things began to happen when I was twelve.

The angels began working overtime.

I was in junior high school, and one day I was sitting in class when I noticed what appeared to be colors around my teacher's head and shoulders. Then an airplane and the word "Philadelphia" came to my mind.

After class, I spoke to him, and he told me that he was flying to Philadelphia.

What was going on here?

Later, I learned that I had seen his aura, or the energy field surrounding all living things. I had begun picking up thoughts from others, intuitively. It was called telepathy, I learned, the most common form of psychic ability. The feeling of "just knowing" something. As time went on, my intuitive sense grew and appeared more frequently. I kept track of things and found that I was right about 80 percent of the time.

I never told this to any of my friends when I was a teenager. But I told my mother. "Don't worry," she told me. "I have that gift, too, and so did my father." So it had been passed on from my grandfather through my mother, and to me. It never scared me, and I never thought it was weird or in any way supernatural. It was just a gift from God.

In the meantime, I was studying hard, playing sports, and having fun as a majorette in high school. During my senior year at Warrensville Heights High, I was a runner-up in the Miss Teenage Cleveland pageant, in which I'd twirled my baton with boundless energy and skill. I looked like the All-American girl, a Barbie doll, with my poufed hair, bright eyes, and big smile.

I was on top of the world. I had a solid grounding in the basics of faith from the Catholic Church; an open mind about spirituality and metaphysics that I got from my mother, my own experiences, and my constant questioning and research; and I was headed for college!

I graduated from high school in 1963, spent one year at the University of Miami, in Florida, then entered Ohio University. I finally began talking about my beliefs and experiences to my friends. My roommates constantly came to me for advice. They wanted to know what their grades would be, or if a boy they liked would call and ask them for a date. I was their Dear Abby. My intuition, my angelic assistance kept growing and becoming ever more accurate. I felt close to God and happy that I could help people.

With a bachelor of science degree in education, I graduated

from Ohio University in 1968 and moved to Fort Lauderdale, Florida, with my family. That year, my father, only fifty-eight, died of leukemia. The bond my mother and I shared grew even stronger.

On occasion during my youth and continuing through my adult years, I'd seen angelic forms. They were like a milky white fog floating at my level, not above me. If this angelic form touched me, it felt warm and tingly, and ultimately very relaxing.

The angels who guided me never gave me the impression that they had names. But I sensed that I had two guardian angels who were with me at all times, one male and one female.

My professional life was mapped out: I would go on to teach physical education. I received my master of science in learning disabilities at the Florida Institute of Technology. I chose as my thesis "The Nutritional Approach to Learning Disabilities." My interest in holistic health had begun in childhood when I searched for a way to cure my migraine headaches. It was this quest that also opened up spiritual doors for me. My migraines were a blessing in disguise.

In my early twenties, I realized that my concept of God had evolved from a limited understanding of who "He" was. I would come to realize that "He" is a vibrating sea of intellectual energy, a cosmic power and infinite intelligence and love. I learned that this Higher Intelligence is known by many different names to many different people. "He" is neuter: neither man nor woman, personal nor impersonal.

I often refer to God as "He" out of habit, left over from my Catholic upbringing. But I never thought that God was a male form. I saw then, and see now, that God is an energy, nondenominational, not limited to any one religion, dogma, ideology, creed, or preconceived idea. Through my studies and travels I realized that we are all created in His image, and should, therefore, strive to not limit ourselves.

My first step in those travels began in 1970 when I decided to go to Japan. I was exploring the concept of reincarnation (I'm still not entirely sure where I stand on that, even now!) and believed that I may have lived at least one previous lifetime in Japan, so spending time there seemed to be a good way of further exploring this.

I would be in a foreign land where I didn't know the language or the people. I would certainly have to depend on the guidance of God and his angels. "Without an itinerary," I told myself, "this will surely test my faith and my communication with God."

Boy, did it ever! There's an exhilaration that comes with following your inner guidance. And that began from the first moments when I envisioned this trip and continued throughout my stay among the Japanese.

Much to my family's and friends' surprise, I abruptly sold my car, quit my teaching job, and bought a one-way plane ticket to Tokyo. I was twenty-five and ready to see the world.

A few days before leaving, my intuition told me that I would meet an important contact for my trip at, of all places, the Benihana of Tokyo restaurant in Fort Lauderdale. Not questioning this rather unusual vision, I went right over.

The angels led me to the right place at the right time. I met two Japanese businessmen at the restaurant who offered to call a sponsor family in Osaka who they were certain would invite me to stay at their home. I hadn't even left American soil, and already my faith in divine guidance was proving correct.

My first month in Japan was spent in Osaka with the sponsor family. I was going about the usual tourist activities: attending the Tokyo World's Fair, going to the opera, the markets, and cultural events. But I was also meditating, praying, and learning about Eastern philosophy.

When I felt it was time to leave Osaka and move on, I took the bullet train to Tokyo.

Not knowing a soul in that city, I meditated in the train station, visualizing that someone who spoke English would come to me and guide me to where I was supposed to stay. Suddenly, I received an impression that I was in the wrong place. I remembered that during my month-long stopover in Hawaii just before I arrived in Japan, I had called Hickam Air Force Base and asked where the largest base in Japan was located. The largest one was in Tachikawa, and the second largest was in Yokohama.

I decided in the train station that one of these would be my destination instead of Tokyo. I sensed that I should go to Tachikawa and boarded the train for the one-hour trip. I knew that I'd be guided to where I belonged.

Arriving exhausted and somewhat dispirited around ten o'clock that night, I stood alone, not knowing a soul at the train station, next to my absurdly large, heavy suitcases, still thinking positively! Knowing that whatever my needs were, they would be met. Knowing this was part of my test of faith, I kept repeating to myself, "I know Infinite Intelligence is guiding me to the right place." I had learned that thoughts are *things*, and with them we can create our own destiny.

I left the train station. Walking through the narrow streets, I heard music coming from a bar on the second floor of a building. It was almost midnight, and I had to get off my feet, so I went inside. I sat down, and minutes later a Japanese girl who looked approximately my age sat down at my table.

"My name is Hiroko," she volunteered. "What is yours?"

"Linda," I answered.

"Where are you staying?" she asked.

I told her I didn't know yet.

She asked me to stay at her house, at least for the night. And where do you suppose she lived? In Tokyo! I had been guided to Tachikawa, in order to find a place to stay in Tokyo.

The two cities were about an hour apart, and Hiroko worked

at the Tachikawa Air Force Base. Another angelic "coincidence." I accompanied her to work on the free bus for military personnel and base workers. At the bus stop, I met an American girl who invited me to her house, where I was greeted warmly by her family.

Her father was a military official in charge of five bases, and he helped me to get military passes so I could travel on military planes and buses and go into all the clubs and shops on base. During the rest of my stay in Japan, I lived with this generous family and volunteered with the Red Cross in the base hospital, taking care of wounded Vietnam War soldiers.

After a year in Japan, I came back to Fort Lauderdale in the summer of 1971, restless because I hadn't found "answers" in Eastern philosophy, just more knowledge that led to more questions.

In trying to pick up the life I had left behind, I went about learning even more about health and spirituality. I decided to continue my profession as a teacher, but I wanted to focus on teaching about holistic living, as a lecturer. I knew I could do even more to help others this way and felt that if my intuitive energies were developed even further, I could be of more help to people.

One hot, humid night that summer I sat alone on the shore of Biscayne Bay, in Miami, facing a crossroads in my life. I knew I had much greater intuitive—psychic—ability than most people: I was clairvoyant, could see auras, and could feel the divine guidance of God and the angels. I had even gone to the mystical Far East in my search for the truths that eluded me. I had prayed in gilded temples and ancient shrines, remote churches and great cathedrals. I had tried to learn everything possible about the people I met. I had tested my faith in many ways. But I felt that something was missing.

I was a normal human being, a young woman who, like most people, was sometimes influenced by the frivolous lifestyles of those around me. Though I had not put my *whole* being into the service of God, I felt that I had still been singled out for a special mission on His behalf. I just didn't know what that mission was, and although I had asked for guidance repeatedly over the last year, I hadn't gotten any clear answers.

I was desperately unhappy that night. The bay heaved and sprayed, its dark waves breaking at my feet; the city's lights danced on its choppy surface. But all I could do at that point was pray. I told God that I was choosing at that moment to release my life to Him; that I no longer wanted anything that was not for my highest good.

"I no longer want to do anything in my life except *your* will," I said.

Suddenly I found myself staring at the water with a new inner peace, as if the emotional catharsis I had just experienced had calmed the bay waters, and my mind.

The following morning I was awakened by a voice.

"Linda, I want to help you," it said.

Startled, I sat up in bed, thinking I had been dreaming.

"We will be working with you, guiding you," the voice continued. "We will present you with many opportunities to help you in the fulfillment of your chosen work."

God had at last responded to my prayers. The voice was of divine origin, I sensed that. Was it one of my guardian angels? Was it another angelic being? Was the voice in the room or in my head? I don't have objective answers to any of those questions.

Since that morning of July 30, 1971, my life has been guided by God and His angelic messengers. I can feel their presence. For those of you who doubt that these forces exist, I can only show you how to experience this communication yourself.

During the last twenty-plus years, I have studied, traveled extensively, and taught people of all ages and backgrounds the holistic principles of a healthy mind, body, and soul. Following our inner guidance system, the divine assistance given by the angelic spirit, is a cornerstone of healthy living.

I am just as comfortable learning from a wise old *kahuna* in the lush mountains of Hawaii as I am talking about the universe with a nun in Los Angeles, a rabbi in Philadelphia, a priest in New Mexico, or an atheist in Seattle. We all have much to learn from one another, many ideas to share.

Through my own radio and television programs, guest appearances on others, and my frequent lectures, I have been fortunate to meet many people with many stories to tell. I am grateful to all of you for enriching my life and the lives of many others.

When I put the word out that I was gathering stories of angelic assistance to include in a book about communicating with angels, people responded from all over the country with letters, phone calls, and even faxes!

These folks are no different from your family, your coworkers and friends. They have all had experiences that made a lasting impression on them, and in some instances changed their lives. They are Christian, Jewish, or of no particular religious denomination. They are doctors, police officers, nurses, homemakers, journalists, schoolchildren, secretaries, business owners, and artists. They are college-educated and have advanced degrees. And they have never gone to college. They live in big cities, in suburbs, in small towns, and out in the country. They are male and female, liberal and conservative and middle of the road.

They're not quite sure what to make of their experiences, and they believe wholeheartedly that their lives are graced by the angels. They've never spoken about this to anyone outside their intimate circle of friends and family. They've never told a soul before now. They've talked about it publicly for years.

They are all telling the truth as they experienced it.

Some have asked to be called by another name, but most are using their real names.

In nearly every story there were witnesses to the experience. The angels, it seems, go about their work freely and openly.

As I lectured around the country about angels, people were eager to open up. When I told of my experiences, they felt comfortable recounting their own. Some of the stories you read here come from people I first met when they came to hear me speak, or heard me interviewed on radio or television. Some come from people who have been my clients. And some are from those who heard through the grapevine about this book, who were referred to me by friends, colleagues, and the media.

It's been wonderful to see this renewal of interest in angels. They've always been with us, and although I don't believe they've been *personally* ignored in our modern world, they certainly have been *publicly* absent outside of church, synagogue, and mosque for the better part of the twentieth century.

But in the last few years, it's clear that angel awareness has blossomed once again. In the bookstores, on the magazine stands, on talk shows, and on news programs—everyone's talking about angel experiences, angel lore, and the rise of interest in anything and everything angelic.

Divine assistance, through angels, is being addressed in relation not only to faith, but also to optimum physical and emotional health. Looking to a Higher Power for guidance and strength has always been the foundation of the twelve-step recovery programs, and now angel power has found its way into some twelve-step practices as well.

Psychoneuroimmunology, the relatively new branch of medicine that focuses on the mind-body connection, even studies angel power.

Ladies' Home Journal, one of the biggest national women's magazines, publishes readers' experiences with angelic assistance.

While angels have been represented in art for centuries, and in the lyrics of popular songs, and in movies and TV programs for decades, more recently angels have also become the subject of seminars and workshops, national conferences and conventions, newsletters and even collectors' clubs.

While I was putting this book together, CBS News announced in the fall of 1993 the results of a nationwide poll: 67 percent of Americans believe in angels, 54 percent believe they have a guardian angel, and 12 percent say they communicate with angels.

"They believe and therefore they see," CBS correspondent Harry Smith said.

A recent Gallup poll shows that 80 percent of Americans believe that God performs miracles. And a study by the National Opinion Research Center, based in Chicago, reports that 57 percent of Americans pray daily, 78 percent pray at least once a week, and only 1 percent never pray.

The angels have played an enormous role in everyone's life, whether they're consciously aware of it or not, whether they call that force angelic or not.

We have only to look around us to realize that some force is guiding our world, for it's simply a miracle that we're here, we're surviving, and we're thriving.

Scientists look for answers and admit that the unknown, the miraculous, the creative force in the universe is elusive. It resists definition. It won't be quantified.

In *The Mind of God*, scientist Paul Davies comments on this quest.

"I began doing research on topics like the origin of the universe, the nature of time, and the unification of the laws of physics, and I found myself trespassing on territory that for centuries had been the near-exclusive province of religion," he notes. "Yet here was science either providing answers to what had been left as dark mysteries, or else discovering that the very concepts from which those mysteries drew their power were actually meaningless or even wrong." Science and religion seek to answer each other's questions every day. They always have and probably always will. "Through my scientific work I have come to believe more and more strongly that the physical universe is put together with an ingenuity so astonishing that I cannot accept it merely as brute fact," he concludes. "There must, it seems to me, be a deeper level of explanation. Whether one wishes to call that deeper level 'God' is a matter of taste and definition."

Can we ever *prove* that there is a God, a Higher Power, a Universal Intelligence, a Creative Force? No one can answer that today. So, by extension, can we *prove* that there are angelic beings or forces? No one can answer that today, either.

The so-called proof is up to each individual's belief. The events are self-evident.

My thanks to all those who so generously gave of their time and their hearts to share their experiences here in these pages.

As the poet Emily Dickinson wrote:

I never spoke with God,
Nor visited in heaven;
Yet certain am I of the spot
As if the chart were given.

Part Two

ANGEL LORE

Bless the Lord, ye his angels,

that excel in strength, that do his

commandments, hearkening unto

the voice of his word.

—PSALMS 103:20

*ELIGIONS AND TRADITIONS* have set up a hierarchy of the angels, a bureaucracy that can confuse us and even distract us from the true nature of the idea of angelic guidance and protection.

There's no need to memorize grand lists of angel names, positions, and duties, because they are not what's important. What's important is far simpler than that. When you cut through the bureaucracy, what you have is a relationship—a one-on-one relationship with the *feelings* that guide you, and those feelings, many of us believe, are our angels.

It's interesting to learn about angel history because it gives us perspective, shows us the long road that faith has taken, and provides a frame of reference and a foundation for our angel awareness.

All native peoples have a faith in the unseen, in the universe, in a power or powers that operate here with us. The only difference is in how each group describes the divine.

Angel lore is rich, varied, and often confusing. Each of the world's major religions that believes in one God has its own version of angel history, organization, and duties, but there is plenty of overlapping, so it's possible to cite generally accepted traditions *within* Judaism, Christianity, and Islam, as well as *among* the three.

Although in America we tend to associate angels with Christianity, most specifically with Catholicism, Christianity didn't invent the notion of angels. Christianity isn't even two thousand years old yet, and it adopted much of its angel basics from other religions thriving in ancient times, primarily Judaism, since Jesus Christ was Jewish.

Christianity and Judaism have in common the Old Testament, in which many references to angels are made. And the angels continue to figure prominently in the New Testament of Christianity. They were always present for the big events in both the Old and New testaments, with messages from God and angelic assistance.

While angels come in many varieties, with different specific duties, these three religions agree that an angel is a *messenger* from God.

And all three agree that the angels were created *before* humans.

As a rule, angels are in a class by themselves. They are not the souls of the dear departed, and in fact have never been human or mortal. They are not the gods of Greek, Roman, or any other mythology. Angels are capable of disguising themselves as humans in order to help us, but they usually don't stick around for very long once their task is completed. You turn your head and they're gone, taking with them whatever vehicle or other useful objects they may have brought with them.

Since we all know that there are exceptions to every rule, you won't be too surprised to hear that there's an exception to this one, too: The ancient scribe and prophet Enoch, very much a human, is said to have been brought to heaven by the Archangel Michael, where God then transformed Enoch into an angel.

Let's begin our journey through angel history with the Essenes, a Jewish sect flourishing as far back as four thousand years ago in the Middle East. The Essenes were still around during the time of Christ, and it is believed that he studied with them during his youth.

The Essenes, a particularly spiritual group that called itself a brotherhood and practiced a more esoteric Judaism than the mainstream, believed in a Tree of Life that had seven branches growing toward heaven and seven roots growing in the earth. The mystical number seven, which is found in other religions and philosophies as well, was further represented by the Essenes in the correspondence between the branches and roots of their Tree of Life to the seven mornings and seven evenings of the week. Their angels were in charge of various themes in heaven and on earth. Under the guidance of a Heavenly Father and an Earthly Mother, these angels were not named. It was only later that Judaism and Christianity gave these angelic vibrations names and physical descriptions resembling familiar human ones. The seven Archangels are based upon the seven Essene angels who worked in heaven and on earth.

In Zoroastrianism, an ancient Persian religion, God had seven special spirits who performed various functions for Him on earth. This religion was filled with angels and influenced ancient Judaism around 1,000 B.C., particularly with the Jewish belief in Judaism's seven special angels, later known in Christianity as the Archangels.

The spiritual and mystical traditions of ancient Judaism thrived for thousands of years. In Judaism it is believed that when God wanted to create man, the angels asked: "What is man that thou art mindful of him? What dost thou seek to get from him?"

God replied, "He will fulfill my Law and my commandments."

"*We* will fulfill it," the angels offered.

"You cannot," said God.

"Why?" they asked.

"It is written: 'When a man dies, you do not die. When a woman bears children, you do not bear children. When a man eats, you do not eat.' "

So it was during God's busy days of Creation that He made very clear to the angels that they were not to be mortal humans. No, God had other things in mind for His angels. They would be with Him in heaven and assist in the orderly running of the universe. They would watch over people, assist them, bring them messages from God.

When a righteous man died, three companies of ministering angels would appear to him, proclaiming his entry into heaven and peace, notes an ancient Jewish teacher, Rabbi Me'ir. Another scholar, Rabbi Phinehas, wrote that there is an angel charged specifically with gathering our prayers and presenting them to God. Second-century rabbi Jose ben Judah taught that angels accompany people on the Sabbath from the temple back to their homes.

The Jewish teachings also point out that the angels are God's family, and that although they do His work, we can pray *directly* to God: "If a man is in distress," it is noted in the Talmud, an authoritative collection of Jewish tradition, law, and theology, "let him not call on Michael or Gabriel, but let him call direct on me, and I will hearken to him straight-away."

Angels were not to be the objects of veneration or adoration; *that* was reserved for God. And even the angels, who live forever, can't see the Glory of God. Only men and women can see God, but never when they're alive, only at the moment of their death.

The original teachings also point out that an angel, acting under God's command, has amazing powers but has no power to cause any harm to a sinner who says, "I repent."

The angels, on behalf of God, have many duties, but most

important, they watch over us on earth. The ancient rabbis tell many stories of miracles: An angel rescues a drowning girl, for example. The Old Testament would put on record many of these occurrences.

It was also believed that "when a man goes on his road, a troop of angels proceed in front of him and proclaim: 'Make way for the image of the Holy One, blessed be He.' " As humans were created in the image of God, the angels loved and protected them, notes mid-second-century rabbi Joshua ben Levi.

The angels do not multiply, according to early Jewish teachings. All the angels who will ever exist *already* exist. And these angels are kept very busy. They visit the sick, and they are present at joyous occasions, too. They come to help, but also to celebrate. And this is *in addition* to the angels that each person has around him or her all the time, the guardian angels. How many guardian angels do we have? The religions do not agree on the answer. According to the original Jewish teachings, each Jew is assigned eleven thousand guardian angels. Christianity doesn't place the number of guardian angels assigned to *any* member of any faith anywhere near that number. Catholics believe that upon our birth we are assigned at least one guardian angel. Christianity doesn't limit the number that we can have. Essentially, we can have as many as God thinks we need.

Considering the turmoil that surrounded the Jews in ancient times, and particularly the persecution that continues into the present in many areas of the world, it's not surprising that each would be assigned eleven thousand guardian angels.

Jewish philosophy teaches that this world is a "university for the soul."

Louis Jacobs notes in *Jewish Ethics, Philosophy and Mysticism* that "Jewish mysticism . . . is a branch of Jewish philosophy, but with greater emphasis on individual experience and a more direct awareness of the divine," and that the mystic "seeks to experience in his personal life those ideas about which the philosopher speaks."

Part of this direct experience with the divine is interaction with God's angels. Since Jewish mysticism is the basis for Christian beliefs about angels, we find that the two schools of thought are compatible. At the root of faith in any religion is a belief expressed by fifteenth-century Jewish philosopher Joseph Albo, who said that we must not think that a thing is impossible simply because the mind doesn't understand its workings.

As God and His angels on His behalf intervene in our lives with everything from coincidences to major miracles, we are reminded of this philosopher's words. The mystic, however, is insatiably curious and wants to *understand* the workings of everything, including the divine.

We often associate mysticism only with the Eastern religions and philosophies, with Buddhist and Hindu thought, with Zen and Taoist meditation and contemplation, or with Native Americans and their vision quests. But mystical Judaism, as practiced more commonly hundreds and thousands of years ago, and to a far lesser extent today, is very similar. While there are certainly differences in approach and methods, the goal is the same: to become one with God. The mystic in Judaism believes that man is literally created in the image of God, so the mystic is described as working to polish himself until he reflects nothing but God.

The mystic doesn't necessarily have to be perceived as some mysterious man. Anyone—man, woman, or child—who seeks knowledge of the divine, and the divine aspect of all things, has a bit of the mystic in him. Anyone who picks up a book about angels has the curiosity of the mystic!

Jewish mystical knowledge, upon which Christian beliefs about God and the angels and the universe grew, is contained in the Kabbalah, which is not a book, but a body of knowledge, of mystical teachings. It was named Kabbalah, which means "tradition," in the twelfth century, but it had been practiced since ancient times, dating back to the time of Moses. Its teachings were handed down orally from generation to generation. It's best understood as a system of thought, a way of perceiving the world and heaven, a way of delving into the mysteries of the universe.

It isn't an intellectual pursuit or a description of religious laws. Nor is it an interpretation of doctrine. It includes meditation and contemplation. And while other spiritual disciplines urge practitioners to engage in their quest by finding a quiet spot on a mountaintop, for example, the Jewish mystic does his contemplation while living in the midst of his community and the world at large. It has been this way since ancient times. Ancient mystics placed quite a bit of emphasis on visions and contemplation. Those in the Middle Ages living in Spain and the Middle East concentrated on prophetic aspects of meditation. European mystics, especially in more recent centuries, prayed intensely.

In Jewish mysticism, for five thousand years, the path has been the same. Perle Epstein notes in *Kabbalah: The Way of the Jewish Mystic* that the seeker "distills God's presence from the stars, people, food—from all life around him. As his senses are further refined, he will become conversant with the ethereal world of angelic beings, pure color and sound, until finally he reaches the unmanifest level of awareness called *devekut*, cleaving to God, the highest state attainable by human consciousness."

The work of the mystic takes place in the mind. To eventually reach the realm of the angels and God, the mystic meditates, contemplates, prays, analyzes, thinks, and visualizes.

One common practice of the mystic is to visualize the journey to God. These visions can best be explained by the metaphor of the Tree of Life, a tree whose branches are made of ten different-colored spheres, each representing an ascending "world" or level of spiritual perception. This tree grows in a garden called the *Pardes*. But before you even get inside the garden, you pass through the realm of the *Ophanim*, angels who take the shape of wheels. These wheels are also represented in the hierarchy of angels that the Christians would later make official in the fourth century.

In *The Book of Direction to the Duties of the Heart*, an influential eleventh-century guide for mystics written by Bahya ben Joseph Ibn Paquda, the spiritual journey to meet the angels in their realm and become one with God takes the seeker through the ten levels of the Tree of Life, each separated by a gate you must pass through.

First gate: Studying the divine in nature. That means every aspect of our earthly world from the simplest organism to humankind.

Second gate: The proper worship of God resulting from these contemplations.

Third gate: Trust. To confide in God alone and trust the divine universal order.

Fourth gate: Acceptance. Growing satisfied with your life, knowing you learn from even the trials of life and that you are in a partnership with God.

Fifth gate: Hypocrisy. Testing your sincerity and faith by tempting you with doubt, anger, and nihilism.

Sixth gate: Humility.

Seventh gate: Repentance. You encounter your past sins, confront your actions honestly, and repent in word, thought, and deed.

Eighth gate: Examination of the soul.

Ninth gate: Abstinence. Self-discipline to be able to abstain from corruption.

Tenth gate: Saintliness.

Upon passing through the tenth gate, the seeker leaves the realm of Awe, being in awe of the divine, and enters into the realm of Love, experiencing the love of the divine.

The mystics were not and are not saying that we can't communicate with angels until we have visions that take us up the Tree of Life, through each gate, and into the lap of God. We interact with our guardian angels and other angels constantly whether we're aware of it or not. All we have to do is need help, for instance, and they're providing it. It may be something we can recognize right away, or not see until much later, but their help is there. Often, we don't even have to *think*, "Oh, wow, I need help here." They're already one step ahead of us, giving assistance.

The mystics are attempting to visualize their way right into the *realm* of the angels and the divine. Indeed, it was after such a series of visions that Enoch, the great ancient scribe, described what the levels of heaven are. It was through these visions that the average guy on the street (or on the dirt path, in ancient times) could learn about heaven, the angels, and God, about their duties, their environment. The mystics who took these spiritual journeys in their minds essentially came back and told the rest of us about what they saw. These visions are the basis for what every Jew and Christian alive today has been taught about heaven.

Enoch, Noah's grandfather, provided the most information. "Following the Jewish mystic pattern to perfection . . . solitude and prayer open his inner eye to the world of angelic beings," Perle Epstein writes in *Kabbalah: The Way of the Jewish Mystic*.

"Soon Enoch is able to commute with ease between the world of men and the heavenly realm of angels. Functioning as a divine messenger, he exhorts mankind to turn away from its worldly preoccupations toward spiritual ones, while his highly developed psychic abilities enable him to learn the divine mysteries directly from the lips of the angels."

Enoch made many journeys to heaven and back and described them in metaphor and great detail. In his last meditative journey of the mind as a mortal, Enoch meets the first order of angels upon entering the heavenly palace. They teach him secrets and he meets the divine quality of *Understanding*, a woman on a throne. Then he meets an aspect of God, whom Enoch described as having a head "white like wool," who is with a being Enoch says is a Messiah, a man whose "face was full of graciousness, like one of the holy angels." Enoch then passes over seven mountains, learns the secrets of lightning and thunder from angels in a valley, and finally meets God, whom Enoch calls the Ancient of Days. As soon as Enoch sees Him sitting on His throne, Enoch is whisked alive into heaven and becomes the angel Metatron.

The Archangel Michael tells Enoch all the secrets of the seven heavens. God is surrounded by thousands, perhaps millions, of angels: Seraphim, Cherubim, and Ophanim. Enoch says: "And my whole body became relaxed, And my spirit was transfigured; And I cried with a loud voice."

The Book of Enoch, three chronicles of Enoch's mystical mind travels to heaven and his descriptions and final transformation into an angel, were compiled around the second century B.C. and remain one of the most vivid descriptions of the angelic realm and the ten heavens.

In the Old Testament, only the angels Michael and Gabriel are mentioned by name. Michael journeyed with the Jews from Egypt and through the desert, gave Moses the Ten Commandments from God, and rescued Daniel from the lion's den.

Gabriel brings many messages to Daniel, among them the prophecy of the coming of a messiah. Later, in Christianity, they are termed Archangels.

The Archangel Raphael first makes his appearance in religious literature not in the Old or New Testament but in the apochrypha Book of Tobit, which relates the story of a man, Tobias, who is assisted by the Archangel Raphael masquerading as a human.

Angels are referred to as holy watchers in some passages of the Old Testament, a reference to the guardian aspect of angelic assistance. In Daniel 4:20, he says "the king saw a holy watcher coming down from heaven."

In the Old Testament, you'll find many instances when angelic qualities are attributed to people. In 2 Samuel 14:17, a handmaid looking for help from King David says, "For as an angel of God, so *is* my lord the king to discern good and bad." She continues her praise for the king's abilities, and in Samuel 14:20 says that King David is "wise, according to the wisdom of an angel of God, to know all things that *are* in the earth."

In the New Testament, Gabriel brings the message from God to Mary that she will give birth to Jesus, and when he is born Gabriel announces the news to the shepherds.

Angels of all kinds make many appearances in the Old Testament.

When Joseph was having second thoughts about Mary because she was pregnant, an angel appeared to him in a dream and said, "Fear not to take unto thee Mary thy wife: for that which is conceived in her is of the Holy Ghost" (Matthew 1:20).

Just after Jesus' birth, King Herod had plans to kill the newborn. Once again, an angel came to Joseph in a dream, this time with a warning and a solution: "Take the young child and his mother, and flee into Egypt, and be thou there until I bring thee word, for Herod will seek the young child to destroy him" (Matthew 2:13).

The angel fulfilled his promise by appearing to Joseph again in a dream: "Get up, take the child and his mother and go to the land of Israel, for those who were trying to take the child's life are dead" (Matthew 2:19–20).

Joseph, Mary, and Jesus went to Israel, but not back to Judea because Archelaus was reigning there after the death of his father, Herod. Afraid that the new king would want Jesus dead, Joseph instead went to the district of Galilee, after having been warned, yet again, in a dream.

The angel's mission is clearly defined in the New Testament's Hebrews 1:14. "Are they not all ministering spirits, sent forth to minister for them who shall be heirs of salvation?"

In Hebrews 2:7, Jesus' stature is explained: "Thou madest him a little lower than the angels; thou crownedst him with glory and honour, and didst set him over the work of thy hands."

One of the most famous quotations about angels can also be found in the New Testament: "Be not forgetful to entertain strangers: for thereby some have entertained angels unawares" (Hebrews 13:2). You never know, do you?

*T*HE CELESTIAL HIERARCHY

With the teachings of the Jewish mystics, the Book of Enoch and other Jewish and Christian writings as a guide, in the fifth century Dionysius wrote the *Celestial Hierarchies*, which is the foundation for today's generally accepted view of the angelic bureaucracy.

Nine orders of angels orbit God's throne, and they are divided into three groups, or triads. Within each triad are three types of angels, called choirs. The first triad is closest to God, followed by the second and the third. The first choir of the first triad is the very closest to God, and so on down the line.

FIRST TRIAD

1. Seraphim
2. Cherubim
3. Ophanim

SECOND TRIAD

4. Dominions
5. Virtues
6. Powers

THIRD TRIAD

7. Principalities
8. Archangels
9. Angels

The Choirs of the First Triad are the assisting angels who always stand before God. St. Thomas taught that these choirs never come to earth. They're also known as God's "faithful angels."

The *Seraphim* have as their chief duty the eternal circling of God's throne while chanting in Hebrew a prayer that is still part of Jewish services today, known as the *Kadosh*. Each Seraph chants, "Holy, Holy, Holy is the Lord of Hosts, the whole earth is full of His Glory." This has been interpreted as a song of creation, and the vibration of Love. These angels are physically described as pure light and thought, and prophets who have seen them in visions say they look like "flaming angels."

The *Cherubim* guard the way to the Tree of Life, east of the Garden of Eden. The Cherub is often thought of as Knowledge. The prophet Ezekiel saw four Cherubim and said they each had four faces and four wings. And yet, although they are most often described this way, painters and artists in the centuries to come would call those pudgy, childlike angels in their colorful works Cherubs or Cherubim.

The *Ophanim*, also known as Wheels or Thrones, are God's transportation. Cherubs would drive these wheels with many eyes and wings in Ezekiel's visions, and Enoch said they looked like "fiery coals."

The Choirs of the Second Triad are the ministering angels who guard the greater things of the universe.

The *Dominions* keep track of the heavenly workforce, regulating each angel's duties.

The *Virtues* provide miracles and work as humankind's cheerleaders, dispensing courage. Two Virtues escorted Christ to heaven and assisted Eve with the birth of Cain. They also bless with God's grace.

The *Powers* guard heaven from demons, and some believe they watch over our souls as we wage the constant battle between good and evil. They also guide those souls who get lost after leaving the body. Because of their continuing battle against evil, some believe that the Powers lost the most angels to Lucifer when he tried to seize control of heaven from God, lost, and then fell to hell, where he rules as Satan, assisted by other fallen angels.

The Choirs of the Third Triad are the ministering angels who give their care more directly to us here on Earth.

The *Principalities* protect religions, nations, and cities.

The *Archangels* are the most important messengers and emissaries between God and humans. Islam recognizes four Archangels, while Judaism and Christianity recognize seven. All are named, have specific duties and qualities, and are often described with human physical characteristics.

The *Angels* are closest to humans and include our guardian angels. In Hebrew, they are called *mal'akh*, which means "messenger." The English word *angel* comes from the Greek *angelos*, which also means "messenger."

The Archangels

Among the countless angels who inhabit the celestial realms are those who have been given names by the world's many religions and cultures. These are the angels we've heard about since childhood, the ones who delighted us and passed along their wisdom not only in the Bible or other religious stories and traditions we studied, but in our popular culture, too.

In the Book of Enoch, three chronicles compiled around the second century B.C., Enoch, chosen by God to write the truth and therefore considered the world's greatest scribe at the time, describes his journey to the heavens. There he witnesses angels in all their bureaucratic glory. He writes of their positions, duties, and characters, their physical appearance and history. He even compiles a Who's Who, naming the seven Archangels, "the holy angels who watch." These seven are generally regarded today as among God's holiest, most trusted angels in both Judaism and Christianity, along with a few others who have made their way onto the list over the centuries.

Enoch, who eventually was taken to heaven and transformed into the powerful angel Metatron, wrote his books while still an earthbound scribe. He lists the seven Archangels as:

- Uriel . . . who is over the world.
- Raphael . . . who is over the spirits of men.
- Raguel . . . who takes vengeance on the world
of the luminaries.
- Michael . . . over the best part of humanity and
over chaos.
- Saraqael . . . over the spirits who sin in the
spirit.
- Gabriel . . . over Paradise and the serpents and
the Cherubim.
- Remiel . . . over those who rise.

Seven Archangels are also mentioned in the Catholic Book of Tobit, where the Archangel Raphael describes them as angels who "stand ready and enter before the Glory of the Lord." The "el" at the end of each angel's name means "shining being."

Dionysius, who in the fifth century wrote *Celestial Hierarchies*, a ranking of angels and heavenly beings that is still generally accepted today, claimed that the Archangels are messengers who carry divine decrees, making them the most important link between God and humankind. They command the angels in heaven, he wrote, and battle the Sons of Darkness.

Only Michael and Gabriel are mentioned by name in the Old Testament. In the New Testament, the seven angels who stand before God in Revelations are widely regarded as the Archangels.

Fifteen famous angels, many of them considered Archangels, have gotten the most attention in angel lore and continue to capture our imagination today.

MICHAEL

Perhaps the most famous and enduring angel of them all, the Archangel Michael is also referred to by Catholics as Saint

Michael. Along with Gabriel, Raphael, and Uriel, Michael is considered one of the great angels. These four always top the list of Archangels in Christianity, Judaism, and Islam. Michael, whose name means "Who is like to God," is said to be closest to God. He is depicted as the heavens' mightiest defender, the angel who led the battle against evil and banished Satan and the fallen angels from heaven.

"Michael is the breath of the Redeemer's spirit who will, at the end of the world, combat and destroy the Antichrist, as he did Lucifer in the beginning," said St. Thomas.

Michael was considered throughout biblical history to be the protector and defender of the Jewish people, journeying with them from Egypt and through the desert. It was Michael who gave Moses the Ten Commandments from God. With the rise of Christianity, Michael became known as "the defender of the Catholic Church." Catholics recite a special prayer to St. Michael the Archangel, asking him to protect them from evil. As the Angel of the Last Judgment, Michael is called for when people are sick, and most important, when death is near. In the Middle Ages, Michael was believed to guide souls to the afterlife. Even today, his angelic spirit is invoked when people of all faiths recite the popular phrase "Glorious St. Michael, Prince of the Heavenly Court, pray for us now and at the hour of our death."

Michael has always been a busy Archangel. He stopped Abraham from sacrificing his son Isaac (although in some traditions the angel Metatron is credited with this deed, too), he appeared to Moses in the burning bush, rescued Daniel from the lion's den, and appeared to Joan of Arc.

In the ancient Essene sect of Judaism, some four thousand years ago, Michael is equated with the Angel of Earth, who regenerates the body. In the Dead Sea Scrolls, he's known as the Prince of Light.

So important was Michael that he was even honored with his

own holiday. The Feast of Michaelmas originated in the Roman Empire in the fifth century, and became even more important in the Middle Ages when Michael was the patron saint of knights. In the Roman Catholic and Anglican churches, Michaelmas is celebrated on September 29. In the Greek, Armenian, and Coptic churches, he's honored on November 8.

In England, it's customary to eat roast goose on Michaelmas, harking back to the days hundreds of years ago when people included a goose in their rent payments to landlords. According to an old English proverb: "If you eat a goose on Michaelmas Day you will never want money all the year 'round." In Great Britain, Michaelmas has traditionally been one of the four quarterly days of the year when certain bills are collected, the beginning of a quarterly court term, and an academic term at Oxford and Cambridge.

The emperor Constantine attributed his victories to Michael's protection and built a church near Constantinople in his honor, naming it Michaelion. The church attracted a flood of pilgrims, many of whom were sick and were said to have been cured by Michael's intervention. So strong was the belief in this chief Archangel's powers from God that churches were built in his honor throughout Europe. Christians in Egypt even dedicated the Nile River to him!

In art, Michael is usually shown carrying an unsheathed sword, but in the Islamic tradition, he is said to have green emerald wings covered with saffron hairs, each containing a million faces and mouths and as many tongues.

In the hierarchy of heavens, the Archangel Michael rules the Fourth Heaven.

On earth, the Old Testament book of Daniel says that it is Michael who will appear when the world is in great peril.

* * *

GABRIEL

Second in importance after Michael, the Archangel Gabriel sits at the left hand of God. Gabriel, whose name means "God is my strength," is the only female Archangel, though the debate continues about his or her gender since she has shown herself as male on occasion, and the male-dominated societies throughout history have been reluctant to accept the possibility and prominence of a female Archangel.

Gabriel has always been associated with conception and birth. Known as the Angel of Incarnation, she foretold to Daniel the coming of a messiah, announced to Mary that she would give birth to Jesus, and told Zacharias that his wife Elizabeth would bear John the Baptist. In the Catholic Church, the Hail Mary prayer is the actual greeting that Gabriel gave Mary upon announcing the miraculous conception: "Hail Mary, full of grace, the Lord is with thee, blessed art thou among women."

Catholic tradition continues Gabriel's role as celestial stork, saying that Gabriel also announced Jesus' birth to the shepherds of Bethlehem and then led the angels when they sang around the baby: "Glory to God in the highest, and peace to men of good will."

Gabriel's emblem is the lily, which symbolizes conception, and it is said that she instructs souls during the nine months they are in the womb preparing to come into the world. The ancient Essenes equated her with the Angel of Life, "who enters the limbs and gives the body strength." Giving life in other ways, she's considered the Awakener, the Angel of Dreams, the Angel of Knowledge, and in the Judeo-Christian tradition the Angel of Annunciation, Resurrection, Mercy, and Revelation.

She rules the First Heaven, where Adam and Eve supposedly lived, the closest heaven to our world, and as such was named the Governor of Eden. As the Archangel in charge of Paradise, she coordinates all of the angels.

In the Old Testament, the prophet Daniel has extensive contact with Gabriel both in visions and while praying, and Daniel, in chapter 10, verses 5 and 6, describes Gabriel as a man "clothed in linen, whose loins *were* girded with fine gold of Uphaz: His body also *was* like the beryl, and his face as the appearance of lightning, and his eyes as lamps of fire, and his arms and his feet like in colour to polished brass, and the voice of his words like the voice of a multitude."

Gabriel has also been seen with 140 pair of wings.

One of the most impressive miracles in the Old Testament, the parting of the Red Sea, is credited to Gabriel's intervention on behalf of God.

In Islam, Gabriel is the Angel of Truth and is never considered female. In their holy book, the Koran, which Gabriel dictated to Mohammed in the year 610, Gabriel, not Michael, enjoys the title Chief of All the Angels.

The Archangel Gabriel, in her capacity as an angel overseer, is known in heaven as Ruler of the Cherubim, and she is also honored as a saint. She is the angel of all good news. Catholics celebrate the Feast of St. Gabriel on March 24.

RAPHAEL

The third most important Archangel, Raphael is the Shining One Who Heals. God gave Raphael the powers of healing and the ability to deliver people from danger. He is not mentioned by name in the Old or New testaments but takes center stage in the Book of Tobit, where we learn the most about this friendly, amusing, and gentle celestial being, known as Chief of the Guardian Angels. In this tale, he comes disguised as a man called Azarias and helps Tobias in many ways during a dangerous journey, revealing only near the end that he is Raphael. He teaches Tobias how to use parts of a fish as medicine, protects him from peril, and even plays matchmaker, finding him a beautiful, virtuous, and wealthy wife.

Also called Saint Raphael, this Archangel's name means "God has healed" or "Medicine of God," and he is credited with healing the wounds of martyrs and comforting them during their ordeals. Considering his great success in protecting Tobias, Raphael is still asked to give protection to travelers. He is also summoned for the sick or injured and many claim that he makes hospital visits.

In the Old Testament, Raphael healed the pain of Abraham's circumcision and gave Noah the Book of the Angel Raziel, which contained not only medical information but all he needed to know to build the ark.

The ancient Essenes' Angel of the Sun, who gives the fire of life to the body, is said to be Raphael. As the Angel of Science and Knowledge, he was also given the task of guarding the Tree of Life in Eden.

Officially, Raphael rules the Second Heaven, and shares management duties as Chief of the Virtues order of angels. Catholics celebrate the Feast of St. Raphael on May 18.

URIEL

Rounding out the highest echelon of Archangels, as one of the Four Angels of the Presence, Uriel confronts the souls of sinners, often having to take them to task for their actions. He's known as the Angel of Repentance, and his name means "Fire of God." His Christian symbol is an open hand holding a flame. This is not an angel you'd want to meet if you've done wrong. He is said to be the Archangel who stood at the gate of Eden holding a fiery sword, and in keeping with his strong image also watches over terror and thunder.

Uriel, though, also has a lighter side, as the Angel of Music, according to Christian traditions. In Islam, Israfel is the musical celestial being, and in Judaism, it's Metatron who's called the

Master of Heavenly Song. Uriel is also the Angel of Poetry.

In the Old Testament, Uriel was sent by God to warn Noah of the flood, and according to Jewish tradition, he gave the mystical Kabbalah to the Jews. He is also the angel who interprets prophecies.

RAGUEL

Raguel means "Friend of God," and as such this Archangel named in the Book of Enoch transported Enoch to heaven. Enoch described him as taking vengeance on the world of luminaries, but that is not meant to imply that Raguel's activities are strictly negative. He does judge his fellow angels and is said to watch over their good behavior as well.

SARAQAEL

Also known as Sariel, the Archangel Saraqael, like Raguel, keeps a watchful eye on his celestial colleagues. Enoch wrote that Saraqael is responsible for the fate of angels who break the Laws. Like Raphael, this Archangel is also a healer, and many believe he taught Moses.

REMIEL

This Archangel also goes by the names Ramiel, Jeremiel, and Phanuel. His name means "God raises up" and "Face of God," both of which refer to his primary duty as the Angel of Hope, who leads souls to Judgment, presiding over souls in the afterlife who await entry into Paradise. Those on their way to heaven are said to be "rising."

He is mentioned in the Kabbalah, the Jewish mystical knowledge that includes the soul's path to God and interaction with angels. As the angel in charge of "true visions," he interprets these for mortals.

METATRON

In mystical Judaism, particularly in the Kabbalah, Metatron is the supreme angel, outranking even Michael. His name means "Closest to the Throne," and in the Judeo-Christian world he is known as Prince of the Divine Face, Angel of the Covenant, and King of the Angels, with the hefty responsibility of being in charge of "the sustenance of the world." His duties overlap with those of the Archangels and other angels. In the Talmud he is the direct link between God and humanity, and in the Kabbalah that power is reflected in Metatron's title, Angel of the Lord.

He is said to have thirty-six wings, in six sets of six, and countless eyes, which he would no doubt need for his mighty and expansive task of watching over the entire world as we know it. In Judaism, Metatron is also the Master of Heavenly Song. As the tallest angel, variously described as between eight and thirteen feet tall, he's quite the imposing figure, and part of his mission is to be ruthless to those who don't obey.

Enoch, the great scribe who wrote extensively of heaven in the Book of Enoch, which was compiled roughly twenty-two hundred years ago, was ultimately whisked off to heaven permanently where God had the Archangel Michael help transform Enoch into Metatron by anointing him with oil and then dressing him as an angel. Since Enoch was revered as a writer, Metatron became the heavenly scribe who records everything that happens in the celestial world.

Where would angel lore be without conflicting interpretations and stories? Metatron's identity is widely accepted as the heavenly manifestation of Enoch, though in some circles, this great angel is said to have been present at the Creation, obviously long before Enoch the scribe walked the planet.

Metatron has a twin brother, Sandalphon, who is said to rule the Fifth Heaven.

RAZIEL

The name Raziel means "Secret of God," and this important angel is known as the Angel of the Secret Regions and of the Supreme Mysteries. He is best known for his Book of the Angel Raziel, not written, of course, in the sense that we on earth write books. You will not find this in any library or archives, for this is where Raziel wrote in the language of angels all the celestial *and* earthly knowledge there is to know.

Legend tells us that he presented this "book" to Adam. From there it ended up in the hands of the aforementioned scribe Enoch, who took portions and incorporated them into his Book of Enoch, which was written by earthly hands. Even Solomon had the Book of the Angel Raziel in his possession. Where it went from there no one—at least not on Earth—knows for sure. An oral version, however, is part of the Kabbalah mystical traditions.

In his book, Raziel unlocked fifteen hundred keys to the mysteries of the universe, but unfortunately they are revealed in angelic language that even some of the greatest angels do not understand.

According to the Zohar, another work of Jewish mysticism, Raziel stands on Mount Horeb every day and tells these secrets to all of humankind.

Raziel also has official duties in heaven, where he is Chief of the Thrones order of angels, and he is most often described as a brilliant white fire.

● ● ●

ANAEL

In the ancient Essene teachings, Anael is associated with the Angel of Air, who breathes air into the body. He rules the Third Heaven and is one of the rulers of the Principalities order of angels.

ZEBUL

Zebul rules the Sixth Heaven by day.

SABATH

Sabath rules the Sixth Heaven by night.

CASSIEL

Cassiel rules the Seventh Heaven, where God lives surrounded by Seraphim, Cherubim, and Wheels.

LUCIFER

Originally God's most beloved angel, Lucifer rebelled, and with many other rebel angels was cast out of heaven. He took up residence in hell, where he is also known as Satan.

MORONI

Moroni, the angel of the Mormons, appeared to Joseph Smith in 1823 in upstate New York and led him to discover and translate writings that became the Book of Mormon. Smith then founded the Mormon sect, the Church of Jesus Christ of the Latter Day Saints.

It wasn't until the fourth century that angels became a major theme in art.

Artists gave their angels wings, therefore making all the orders look pretty much the same, it is believed, just so they would be distinguished from the people in the drawings, paintings, and sculpture.

For hundreds of years following, angels and angel lore were all the rage in cultural and artistic circles. Museums are filled to the rafters with religious artworks, particularly from the Middle Ages through the Renaissance, and many of these incorporate or focus on angels.

Angels were also all the rage in religious circles, particularly within the Catholic Church.

Saints spoke about them frequently and included them in their writings. St. Clement, St. Gregory the Great, Origen, and other Christian sages taught that every country, city, town, village, and family has a guardian angel.

It is believed that the Archangels Michael, Rapahel, Gabriel, and Uriel, who are jointly in charge of the guardian angels, also oversee the nations, states, and cities. The guardian angels, whether they be of entire geographical groups of people, or of individual people, have also been called the Watchers.

A specific angel was believed to watch over each hour, each day, each night, each month, and each season.

Angels were also assigned to other specific areas, including: Matriel, Rain; Sahaquiel, Sky; Shalgiel, Snow; Ramiel, Thunder; Gabriel, Dreams; Yroul, Fear; Zadkiel, Memory; Rampel, Mountains; Achiaih, Patience. St. Thomas taught that each star, planet, sun, and other heavenly body has an angel to prevent disorder among the millions that whirled through space.

Jews and Christians alike believed that the most important object of the angels' care is the human race, and that each of us is appointed a guardian angel at birth to guide and assist us throughout our earthly lives.

St. Cyril said, "We have nothing to fear from the powers of darkness, for it is written: The Angel of the Lord will encamp round those who fear Him and deliver them."

It wasn't until the twelfth century, in Spain, that the name Kabbalah was given to the Jewish mystical teachings and experiences, which included plenty of angel lore, since the path to God involves angelic assistance. Jewish philosopher Ibn Gabriel named the teachings Kabbalah, which comes from the Hebrew, meaning "to receive." It is also translated as "tradition."

One of the many teachings of the Kabbalah focuses on the ten angels or divine attributes of the universe: Foundation, Splendor, Eternity, Beauty, Power, Grace, Knowledge, Wisdom, Understanding, and Crown. These ten angels are encountered in the journey through the Tree of Life.

In the thirteenth century, also in Spain, Moses de Leon brought the Zohar to the attention of the world. This lengthy mystical commentary on the Torah also includes other teachings. Zohar, which means "light," is also referred to as the Book of Splendor, and is still considered one of the most important of the few kabbalistic teachings to be written down.

When Moses de Leon unveiled the Zohar, he said that it had been written by the second-century teacher Rabbi Simeon ben Yohai, from special mysteries revealed by God. Among those mysteries are the *higher worlds*, those spiritual worlds hidden from human beings, and *revealed worlds*, such as our own on Earth. The Zohar points out that we can't understand our world except in terms of the others because they are so intertwined.

✳

Mystic philosophy went underground in Judaism in the seventeenth century, then reemerged in the eighteenth as the Hasidic movement in Eastern Europe. The most striking difference between this movement and those that practiced contemplation in previous centuries was availability. The Hasidim made their mystical teaching available to the masses rather than limiting it to a chosen few scholars.

In Christianity, angels and other religious figures were no longer the most popular subjects for artists, but they remained in the hearts, minds, and teachings of people even as churches were no longer dominating government in many Western countries.

Angels enjoyed the most attention in Catholicism, where the Archangels had also been named saints. Catholic children were encouraged to pray to the angels, asking for divine protection and assistance.

Visions of angels had come to Joan of Arc back in the fifteenth century, sending her on a mission to free France from the English. In the late eighteenth century, while fighting for American independence from the British, George Washington reported that he, too, had seen an angel.

By the twentieth century, though, skepticism had taken hold. If you weren't a priest, nun, minister, or rabbi, and claimed to have seen or felt the presence of an angel, or to have been given angelic assistance, you'd likely be met with a chuckle at best, or simply called crazy. Even clergy who claimed such assistance were often brushed off by the masses as religious fanatics. Ironically, though, even the most skeptical believed, however privately and quietly, that some unseen force, a guardian angel, kept them from harm and guided them through life.

In recent years, we've rediscovered angels, angel lore, and the angelic presence in our lives. Of course that doesn't mean that the angels ever left. They've been there all along; it's just that *we* have been taking credit for *their* work, or calling it by another name, like coincidence, synchronicity, serendipity, intuition, hunch, or instinct.

In days gone by, people who had angelic experiences were respected and revered, considered holy men or women, blessed by the divine, or at least lucky. Now, with the approach of the twenty-first century, as we look inward again and focus on the spirituality in our lives, and in our universe, we realize that we have *always* been blessed.

Part Three

ANGEL AWARENESS

✳

For we walk by faith, not by sight.

—2 CORINTHIANS 5:7

✳

*A*NGELS LOOK FOR AN OPENING in our consciousness, then they slip into our thoughts, or our dreams. But they can also arrange events, provide people and circumstances to assist us, or even show up themselves in light or humanlike form.

Parts Three and Four are filled with angel experience stories from people all over the country. Many of them illustrate the angel questions asked in these sections, so you'll be able to see angel assistance in action as you learn more about angel power.

We'll look at the many ways we communicate with the divine, and what part faith plays in our lives.

While there may be plenty of other evidence of angelic assistance, we humans are notoriously skeptical of what we cannot see with our very own eyes.

"Angels speak. They appear and reappear. They feel with apt sense of emotion. While angels may become visible by choice, our eyes are not constructed to see them ordinarily any more than we can see the dimensions of a nuclear field, the structure of atoms, or the electricity that flows through copper wiring," Billy Graham has said. "Our ability to sense reality is limited: The deer of the forest far surpass our human capacity in their keenness of smell. Bass possess a phenomenally sensitive built-in radar system. Some animals can see things in the dark that escape our attention. . . . So why should we think it strange if men fail to perceive the evidence of angelic presence?"

Joan Borysenko, a renowned psychologist and scientist at the forefront of psychoneuroimmunology, the branch of medicine that studies the mind-body connection, believes that spirituality is a key to healing, and she has a personal relationship with the divine.

"I think divine help comes in different ways for different people," she has said. "I believe in the angelic realm, so one of the things that I do every day is invoke the angels."

She follows a practice from an ancient Jewish prayer, in which she first invokes the Archangel Michael on her right side. Since he's the angel of love, she asks for his help in being "truly lovable and loving," she says.

Then, on her left side, she invokes the Archangel Gabriel, who helps us overcome fear. In front of her she invokes the Archangel Uriel, the angel of a clear mind, and behind her she invokes the Archangel Raphael, the angel of healing.

To invoke angels, she says, is simply to *recognize their presence*.

After invoking the angels, Borysenko imagines divine light coming from above, into her heart, and flowing through her body. That light, she points out, is called the *shekina* in mystical Judaism—the divine feminine in creation—and is the part of the divine that lives within each of us. She finishes up with unity and protection prayers.

"What's been tremendously helpful for me," she has said, "is the recognition that help is all around us, but that we're going to sit here stewing in our own fears unless we ask for that help. And when we're willing to ask for help, help is forthcoming."

No matter what your religion, or if you have one at all. No matter how you communicate with the divine and the angels. No matter what form the evidence of angelic assistance takes.

𝒜NGEL FACTS

- Angels can speak. They can appear and reappear. They feel with a keen sense of emotion.
- Angels can become visible by choice.
- Angels can appear in any form our imagination will accept.
- If you believe, expect powerful angels to accompany you in your life experiences.
- Angels are not omnipresent: They can only be at one place at a time.
- There is no limit to the number of angels who will come to your aid.
- Angels can appear as dazzling, almost blinding white light.
- Angels do not control us, and they do not learn our lessons for us. They have the ability to inspire us and send us messages that help us with all aspects of our lives.
- Angels are very creative in the ways they communicate with us, but we have to listen.
- Angels have a great sense of humor.
- Angels inspire us through insight and sudden brilliant ideas.
- When you open your awareness of them, angels will begin to appear in every area of your life.
- Angels are light and playful as well as serious.
- Your quest to communicate with your angels and be open to them begins in your own heart.
- Our guardian angels stay with us after death, guiding us, going over the lessons we've learned, and assisting our souls as we prepare to move on.

How and Why Do Angels Come to Us?

Psalm 91 answers that question quite simply, beginning with verse 11:

> *For he shall give his angels charge over thee,*
> *to keep thee in all thy ways.*
> *They shall bear thee up in their hands,*
> *lest thou dash thy foot against a stone.*
> *Thou shalt tread upon the lion and adder:*
> *the young lion and the dragon shalt thou trample under feet.*

The angels, on behalf of God, can assist us in *any* way we need it.

> *Because he hath set his love upon me,*
> *therefore will I deliver him.*

As God says in the above verse, He and His angels help us because we have faith and love; we *believe*.

> *He shall call upon me, and I will answer him:*
> *I will be with him in trouble;*
> *I will deliver him, and honour him.*

In this verse, God continues His simple explanation. We have only to ask for help, and He'll be there. He often does this with the assistance of His angels.

Whether you call this universal force God, the Higher Power, Fate, or *whatever*, it's hard to ignore that *something* out there is intimately connected to us, and that this force isn't necessarily as "out there" as we've always thought, that it is essentially *in* each of us.

Throughout history we've seen examples of the variety of

ways that angels assist people. It's one thing to hear ancient tales, but as dramatic and historical as they are, they can sometimes give the false impression that the angels only help great religious leaders or famous historical figures. It's quite another to hear about modern angelic assistance, just as dramatic as the days of old, but happening in our own backyards and to regular people just like you and me. The angels, as you'll see, are with *all* of us, *all* the time.

Andrew L. Goldman, a thirty-eight-year-old police chief in Missouri, considers angels his silent (and sometimes not so silent) partners.

"That's how I stay alive," he says plainly. "They protect me."

Looking back over his career, particularly the early years as an officer on an urban police force where he routinely dealt with some of the most unsavory characters on the planet, he says that "there were many times I shouldn't have survived. But whom should we give the credit to? The grace of God, ESP, good street sense, or a combination of the three? The bottom line is many times you sense that something had to be a certain way for me to come out of it okay. Looking back I see sometimes that it was divine intervention."

His friends and colleagues call him Andy, and this five-foot-five, 225-pound bulldog of a man—tough, articulate, well-read—puts all ego and take-charge attitudes aside when he tells two very different stories of angelic assistance. The first illustrates his angel-as-police-partner theory, and the second reveals a certain sweetness as he tells how the angels led him to meet his wife.

✳

When I was a younger cop, working in a rather tough section just outside of St. Louis, I'd go up on the highway and sit in my police cruiser in the parking lot of a theater. It gave me a great view, and I'd have my lights on so I could see into the passing cars. I was looking for the proverbial "bad guys."

One night, I see this car go by with three guys in it. Something tells me to stop the car. So I pull behind it, waiting for a traffic violation so I could stop them for something. But they're not doing anything wrong. Still, I have this hunch that something's not quite right about these people. The only thing I can see that's amiss, that's a valid reason for pulling them over, is that the little license plate light is out! Well, that's a violation, so I stop them.

The driver has no license. The passengers have no ID, but they all give me their names. They're not acting like they have anything to hide, they're not nervous, or menacing looking. But I still have this hunch. I radio the information in, but I look at my watch and I know that we're right at a shift change back at the station. I know that the guy running the names through the computer is itching to get home. So I wonder, am I going to get a complete report on these three guys, or is the computer guy going to take shortcuts so he can go home?

I'm waiting for them to radio back with a report, and something tells me that the driver's name is real, but the passengers have given me fake names. The dispatcher radios me back and tells me that all three of the guys are okay—none of them are wanted.

But this internal thing keeps telling me to take the driver in.

"You're under arrest," I tell the driver.

"For *what*?" he asks.

"For not having a light on your license plate," I tell him.

He's flabbergasted. I can hardly believe I'm doing this myself, but I need a reason to bring him in because I sense he's bad news, and this license plate light is the only thing I've got.

I cuff him and take him in, and radio in to have the car towed.

Back at the station I take him over to a police cadet to be booked. Everybody in the room thinks I'm nuts. I go up to communications and the night shift has just come on. I ask the new dispatcher to run the names again. I just *knew* the other one wanted to go home and hadn't run a complete check. So this dispatcher runs it, and I'm watching, and as soon as she hits the enter key on the driver's name, up on the screen it flashes—Wanted: Murder, First Degree. I take a hard copy off the computer, smile and say thank you, and take it to the cadet who's booking the driver.

"Read it and weep, kid," I say to the cadet.

The whole room just stops. These other cops can't believe it.

The cadet looks straight at me and says, "Andy, I'll never question you again."

Now, I'd like to take complete credit for that, and say that I'm a great cop with great instincts, but I don't think the credit is all mine. I think people have better lives when they surrender them. Man, in his arrogance, thinks he's in control. Of nature, of everything. The audacity of man to presume that he is the master of his surroundings, much less the master of his fate, is simply amazing. God, or a higher power, is part of this orchestration, and we can't forget that.

When I ask God for help, it's up to Him—or Her—if He does it directly or sends an angel. And you have to have good intent when you ask for something. Ask by saying to God, "If it's your will, God, I'd appreciate it. If not, well, that'll be fine, too."

Often, of course, God will give us what we need, and guide us, before we've even had a *chance* to ask.

I think the angels led me to meet the woman who would become my wife. And I wasn't even looking or asking.

I graduated from high school in Maryland and, at seventeen, went to work two jobs before going to college. During the day I worked for a shoe company, and at night I worked at a garden center.

It was June 21, 1973, the first day of summer—Midsummer's Night Eve, a magical night, like in Shakespeare. I was going to stay home. It was 7:30 P.M., I took a shower and got into bed. I was *so* tired.

I heard a voice in my right ear. It wasn't in the room, it was in my head.

"Get up," it said. "Go to Bel Air and find Uncle Billy." That was a nickname we called my friend Bill.

I turned over to fall asleep, but the voice came back.

"Get up," it said. "Go to Bel Air and find Uncle Billy."

I turned over. I didn't want to get up. I was exhausted and just wanted to go to sleep. But the voice was pretty persistent.

"Get *up*!" it said, again. "*Go* to Bel Air and *find* Uncle Billy!"

"Okay, okay, *okay*," I finally said, out loud.

I got up, got dressed, and was heading out the door when my father, who knew I was going to bed early, said, "I thought you were sleeping. Where are you going?"

"I don't know why," I replied, "but I'm going to Bel Air to find Uncle Billy."

I got into my car and drove the few minutes to Bel Air, and circled around the center of town three times, looking for Uncle Billy. I felt ridiculous. I didn't even know where he was that night. Well, anyway, I finally pulled into a fast food place, and all of a sudden in drives Billy!

"Follow me," he said out his window.

I followed him, and we drove around town and then parked our cars in a parking lot.

"Get in," he said. "We're going to a party."

I looked inside his car and saw a bunch of our friends, and this blonde girl I recognized from high school but had never met. We drove to the party, which was outdoors in a field. Sue and I walked off alone, under the full moon, and talked all night. We fell in love that night. I knew that night, quite literally, that we would spend the rest of our lives together.

Much later, I learned that that night as she was getting dressed for the party, she had said to herself, "Tonight I'm going to meet the man I'm going to marry."

We were married two years later, almost to the day, on June 19, 1975.

When Andrew L. Goldman listened to his angelic "hunch," he was following one of the most common forms of angelic assistance, one that is prevalent among people who work in life-and-death situations.

Many police officers have told me stories similar to Andrew's during my twenty years of traveling the country teaching. Although each circumstance is different, the angels' methods are the same.

It's interesting to note here, too, that there are other angels at work in law enforcement besides the police officer's angels. A person in need of police assistance or protection has a band of angels helping the police, too.

Casey Brennan, my former personal assistant, is a bright young woman who has a strong relationship with her angels. Her varied experiences with them show both the serious and light sides of their assistance, as she explains.

After reading about angels, I decided to try to talk directly to them. I had never approached them that way before. I was in an unfulfilling relationship at the time, yet I didn't feel I had any reasons to get out of it—unhappiness didn't count, for some odd reason. I asked my angels to send me signs, showing me if this relationship was worth saving, or if I should just pack my bags and leave. Sure enough, the signs came, one by one. I would find evidence of unfaithfulness, after asking the angels for help. It took quite a few other signs for me to get the message, but I'm very thankful to my angels for responding to my call, and for being patient with me.

In less serious instances, I remember a few occasions when my angels have quietly answered my call. I was trying to get through on a business call to a particular company and the line had been busy for quite a while. I kept pushing the redial button over and over again, until I finally said out loud, "Angels, angels please help me get through!" The next time I pushed the redial button the phone rang.

Often faxes wouldn't go through correctly, so I began calling on my fax angel. Now, whenever I do that, my fax goes through without a hitch!

Visualizing angels as well as asking for assistance has been a powerful tool for me. One night I had a migraine headache that wouldn't go away no matter what I tried. So I visualized a beautiful angel floating above my head, with her wings massaging the pain away. As I visualized this, I asked the angel to relieve my headache. Within five minutes my pain was gone.

Feeling lonely and in need of a companion, I decided to write my angel a letter, asking for the perfect mate for me. I listed all the qualities in a man that I needed, not leaving a single detail out. One month later, I met the man I had written to my angel about. He had all the wonderful qualities I mentioned in my angel letter, and I'm happy to say that we're experiencing a beautiful, loving relationship together.

Perhaps the strangest, but lightest, experience I've had recently with angels occurred when I was flying into Fort Lauderdale from my previous home in the Pacific Northwest. A woman whom I had never seen would be picking me up at the airport. I had forgotten to ask for a description. How would I know her? Just as I was thinking that, while I was sitting in the plane thousands of feet in the air, a stewardess walked down the aisle, past my seat. She was carrying a sweater over her arm, looking for its owner. On the sweater was a beautiful angel pin.

At that moment, I knew that the woman picking me up at the airport would also be wearing an angel pin. I was certain of it. And that's how I'd recognize her. Sure enough, when I got off the plane and walked into the airport, among all the many people standing there waiting for passengers, I saw a friendly looking woman wearing an angel pin. She was waiting for *me*.

When Casey wrote a letter to her angel describing her perfect mate and asking for him to appear, she was doing something that has proven quite useful to people in every kind of thought-provoking situation.

It's important that we clear things up in our minds as we ask for angelic assistance, and one of the best ways to do that is to get your thoughts on paper. Writing a letter to your angels or to someone else's angels can help you order your thoughts, weed through them, put them in perspective, and clarify them.

Casey also found out that the angels will always let us know when they're around. The angel pin she saw on the sweater that the flight attendant carried was a sign that her angels heard her request. The angels can show their presence in any number of ways, providing signs and coincidences that don't have to refer

to the word *angel* or any angel symbolism, although they sometimes do. I've noticed that when I ask for the angels' presence
to be known, then things *really* start to happen.

Under What Circumstances Should We Call upon Them?

When it comes to receiving assistance from the universe, there
are no rules.

Your guardian angels are always with you, and others are
available for extra assistance. They can intervene on your behalf whether you ask for them or not.

Certainly when you're in trouble, you may ask for assistance.

Even with little things that may seem insignificant to others,
but are important to *you*, you can call upon the angels.

Whether it's serious or lighthearted, you can *always* ask for
help.

Emily is a newspaper columnist who lives with her husband
and three children in a metropolitan area in the South. She had
an extraordinary experience that she shares in her own words.

First, you must understand that I would not trivialize this story
for the world. I credited this occurrence to divine interference,
but I'm willing to assume an angel was delegated to deal with
my immediate needs.

We were on our honeymoon in July 1979, American Reform
Jews studying serious Orthodox Judaism in the very religious
Mea Sharim neighborhood of Jerusalem and living in the Jew-

ish quarter of the old city.

I went back and forth by bus. One day, after leaving classes, I picked up some groceries: a few onions, a few tomatoes, a chicken, and a handful of other things. Then I got on the bus.

It took about twenty minutes to get to the bus stop nearest our apartment, the end of the route, adjacent to the holy Western Wall. Each day, I got off the bus, walked right past the wall, and climbed a set of stairs to reach the courtyard where we lived.

On this particular day, I stood up to leave the bus and my groceries crashed to the floor around me. The chicken had leaked, destroying the brown paper bag. If I had been at any other bus stop on the planet, I would have simply bundled my groceries into my skirt, hiked it up, pouchlike above my knees, and made do. But I was at the wall. I could not walk past the wall with my skirt pulled up above my knees. I wasn't Orthodox yet, but I had already come that far.

I crawled around the floor of the bus, gathering my goods. Then I said, half aloud, half to myself, more cursing than praying, "God, I wish I had a shopping bag!"

At that moment, I looked under the seat in front of mine to reclaim an onion that had fallen from my lap, and there was a beige plastic shopping bag with a brown mesh pattern. It would hold everything. I filled it up and took it home.

When you are given a shopping bag by an apparent Jerusalem-induced miracle, you try to hang on to it. But when I looked for that shopping bag just a day or two later, it was gone.

Emily's story is a classic example of "ask and you shall receive." So often, it's just that simple. Hundreds of times I've needed something and the angels have provided it. When we open our awareness, we'll begin to notice all the help we're receiving.

I'd like to tell you what happened to me a number of years ago when I simply *asked*.

Since I wasn't involved in a relationship at the time, it seemed like the perfect opportunity to visualize the qualities I was seeking and ask the angels for help. As part of the list I drew up, I included what I considered to be "my type" of man physically. I chose a handsome man who appeared in a catalog. Now, I didn't expect to meet this man, but his appearance was what I was focusing on. This model looked like the kind of guy I'd find appealing.

Not long after, I went to a restaurant to meet friends. Almost as soon as I walked in the door, a very handsome, charming young gentleman introduced himself to me. We sat down and spoke for a while, and he asked me on a date. I felt that it was okay to have dinner with him, that he was safe. So I did. I found out that he was a businessman from the Midwest as we both talked about our life's work. Back in the living room of his hotel suite, where we'd stopped briefly, I noticed on his coffee table the same catalog that I had at home—the one that I clipped the photo from.

"That's me," he said, pointing to the photo of the dream man I had put in my wish list at home. "I also model on the side."

I was in shock. I hadn't recognized him as the man in the catalog. And I couldn't believe that I was out on a date with the man from my wish list!

All these years later, I still am amazed that the angels arranged for us to meet.

So, yes, it is possible to be brought together with exactly what or who you've asked for. But what happens after that isn't guaranteed. You're given an opportunity and what's best for you will follow.

✳

August Priest, a massage therapist in Arizona, often asks for spiritual guidance when he's employing one of his many healing techniques. He usually uses acupressure and Native American methods for physical and emotional healing, but one day he was introduced, by his angels, he says, to something entirely different.

"A client of mine had a six-month-old daughter who was very bonded to her. She cried when anyone else held her," August recalls. "Her mother asked me to hold her for a minute while she tended to something in the house, and I wasn't sure what to do."

To keep the baby from crying, August asked for spiritual guidance.

"The next thing I know, I'm making this loud sound, like whale song or the blowing of a conch shell. It was what I felt I should do."

He couldn't believe what he saw.

"I turned the baby around and she wasn't crying, she was cooing!"

He had never practiced sound toning before, but later learned that it was a valuable healing technique.

"The vibration helps especially in healing emotional things," he discovered. "It's very calming."

August has used this technique hundreds of times with his clients since he quieted a crying baby four years ago and has found that "everyone responds in some way because of the vibrations."

With each client, he says, he does what he did that first time. "I just let my intuition, my angels, guide me."

As August discovered, the healing angels work through us. They work through our hands, allowing us to heal others and heal ourselves. They can also work through music and scent to prompt healing, through walking and deep breathing—literally anything that will facilitate our physical, emotional, and spiritual healing.

In addition to following the proper diet and lifestyle to help prevent devastating headaches, I call upon the angels to heal my migraines, and have for many years. We work together. I remember the turning point very clearly: I was in much pain, and had been for weeks, and nothing I did or the doctors did could relieve this debilitating migraine. I cried out for help from the angels, and then suddenly felt calm and warmth as I heard a voice say: "You will never have to suffer like this again."

Although I've had periodic migraines since then, they were right: I never suffered like that again, and they continue to heal me.

Darline Beck, a retired Fort Lauderdale secretary, has told me about her angel experiences for many years. This particular story illustrates how playful angels can be, as Darline tells it in her own words.

My twin sister, Arline, and I have always believed in guardian angels and have asked for their guidance. One day, Arline, a flight attendant, had been looking for her uniform wings for at least a half-hour with no luck. Our mother joined the search, but still no luck. Panic time! It would soon be time to leave for the Miami airport, so I pitched in to help. I couldn't find the wings, either.

"Let's ask Herbert to help us. He was so wonderful about keeping track of your purse, keys, and wings," I said, referring to her late husband. "Maybe he can find your wings. Where do you keep his ashes?"

She walked to the cabinet where his ashes were, opened the door, and lo and behold, there were her wings!

"But Mother and I already looked here," my sister said, shocked at her discovery. "And they weren't here before!"

Were they there all the time? Did they just materialize there at that moment? We don't know.

"Thank you, Herbert," we all yelled out, loud and clear.

We felt the smile on his face as he shook his finger at us.

Was Herbert responsible for this, or our guardian angels, or both?

I give thanks to my many angel friends and guides and always give thanks to God for all things. And as I get less hesitant to talk about angels to others, it's wonderful to hear other stories. More people than we realize have had angel experiences but are hesitant to share them for fear that someone might call them crazy. But, you know what? As for me, no one ever has.

What Can They Do for Us?

Although you may find this hard to believe, they can do anything they *want* to do for you. As God's messengers, they're not limited.

Now, having said that, I must list some of the exceptions to that rule! They are here to assist and to do *good*. They will *not* act as your avenging army. They will *not* harm people for you. They will *not* force people to do anything against their will. They may enlighten people to change their minds, but force is out of the question.

They can do some pretty remarkable things. They can move a car so that it won't hit you. They can arrange an infinite number of coincidences and synchronicities so that you'll be at the right place at the right time, and so that you'll receive what you *need* from any given situation or person. They can bring anyone or anything into your life that you really *need*, so long as it doesn't involve working against someone's will or working in a negative way. They can work miracles.

Leigh, a journalist in her late thirties, has always relied heavily on her intuition and instincts, both as a professional and in her private life.

Since childhood, she's been blessed with an uncanny sixth sense and has felt that she has been guided and helped by guardian angels. She has looked at this as a partnership more recently, she says, and wonders if that has come with the wisdom of maturity.

Leigh has had many experiences that can be interpreted as the intervention of angelic assistance—dramatic, practical, and humorous—and she has chosen some of the more memorable ones to share here.

On the day she began compiling these stories, she called me, laughing.

"You won't believe what I just saw," she said. "Well, actually, you probably *will* believe it."

"What was it?" I asked.

"I just came back from running errands, and as I drove out of the bank parking lot a car drove in, passing me. It caught my eye at first because it was so bland looking. Light gray, kind of boxy, maybe ten years old. An older woman with white hair was driving. She had on a pink sweater, which was odd since it's so hot outside. She looked like she'd just come off the set of *The Waltons*—very sweet and grandmotherly, like she'd serve tea and cookies, and have lace doilies all over her house. But it was her license plate that got me. It wasn't a novelty item, it was the real thing. And it didn't have any numbers on it, just letters. You know what it said?"

"No, what?" I replied.

"AN ANGEL," Leigh said simply. "I guess I don't even have to ask if that was a sign, do I? I smiled all the way home, feeling like the universe had winked at me."

The universe has a way of doing that, doesn't it?

Perhaps that license plate crossing Leigh's path when it did was an acknowledgment from God, from the angels, a way of saying *Thanks for sharing your experiences with others.*

For almost fifteen years, Leigh's work has been published regularly in the country's most prestigious magazines and newspapers. Often, she says, while she is interviewing people, the conversations turn philosophical. She's been pleasantly surprised to find that nearly all of the literally hundreds of people she's interviewed have expressed spiritual interests and beliefs.

"Artists, musicians, dancers, writers, those who create *always* speak about their talent and inspiration with such awe. They consider it a gift from some spiritual realm," she says. "The artist's muse is an angelic concept. And those in the sciences, they're some of the most fascinating because they're grappling with the duality of belief versus proof. Some feel that science is now creeping into the territory once reserved for mystics— that physics, for example, is close to proving, at least theoretically, the unity that philosophers and mystics have been talking about for centuries."

Leigh's angel experiences are told here in her own words. They range from childhood experiences to more recent ones, from personal to professional. In each, you'll see the universe not only winking back, but lending quite a helpful hand.

✳

I was raised in an upper-middle-class home in the Northeast, with a typical religious upbringing for a Conservative Jewish family: more cultural than religious. We received the standard religious education at Sunday School and Hebrew School (twice a week after regular school), and celebrated the major holidays. Of course, I was also exposed to all the Christian traditions through my friendships with my friends of various religions, and school, where we always sang Christmas carols in choir. In our holiday programs we also performed Hannukah songs every year, usually the well known *dreidel* songs about the spinning tops kids play with. So I had a pretty well-rounded education. And, as an intensely curious child, I always wanted to know *more*, about *everything*, no matter what the topic.

I think I was lucky to be exposed to so much. I knew how to make chicken soup, but I also knew how to decorate a Christmas tree. On Christmas Eve we'd visit friends who'd invite us to hang the ornaments, toss the tinsel, and sip hot chocolate. I had a pretty strong interest in history, so I learned about religions in a historical context, too, not just from a celebration aspect. I knew that Christianity was not just Santa Claus and the Easter Bunny. I knew that Judaism was more than lighting candles at Hannukah or eating *matzoh* on Passover. The philosophy and mysticism of the Eastern religions fascinated me. I was probably an armchair philosopher by the time I was six.

But, when I thought about angels, I always thought about Christianity—Catholicism in particular. Despite my Jewish education, I really had no idea that angels played any part in Judaism. Our teachers never addressed it. As I got older I realized that the mystical part of Judaism is only truly alive in the Orthodox branch, among the most observant Jews, and the ultra-Orthodox, the Hasidim, whom you can easily recognize because of their resemblance to the cast of *Fiddler on the Roof*.

In Conservative and Reform Judaism, a modern, watered-down version of Orthodox or traditional Judaism, mysticism and spirituality was glossed over. Too bad, I thought then, and still do now, because that's the most fascinating aspect of *any* religion. I would be an adult before I even found out that angels aren't the exclusive property, so to speak, of Christianity, that, in fact, angels ended up in Christian religious lore as a carryover from Judaism. That angels are as prominent in Judaism as Christianity. That that's where they began: in the Old Testament. Ancient and contemporary Jewish writings are filled with references to angels. Other Jewish people I knew were as surprised to find this out as I was! The mystical parts of Judaism have traditionally been hush-hush. In Orthodox circles, it was long recommended that men not even study the Kabbalah, the body of Jewish mystical knowledge, until they are forty years old and wise enough to understand it. Historically, women have never been encouraged to study the mystical aspects of Judaism.

When I was only eleven, I decided for myself that I wasn't too keen on organized religion, that instead it was going to be just God and me. A personal, simple religion based on faith, not culture or ritual. I continued to absorb information like a sponge, but I had carved out my own spiritual identity separate from any particular organized religion. It was simple. It was pure. I liked the idea, and still feel enormously comfortable with my beliefs. In fact, I've always thought that organized religion, the institutions, can get in the way of faith, put too much complication between the individual and God.

When I was a child, my life was filled with intuition, coincidence, synchronicity, and the like. I knew that I was some kind of receiving station for information—information that came to me mostly spontaneously; I didn't ask for it specifically the great majority of the time. And mostly it was outside the realm of my five senses. I didn't have to see, hear, touch, taste, or smell as proof of something. Mostly, I just *knew* things, knew them instinctively or intuitively. I was rarely wrong about these things.

As you can imagine, this came in quite handy for a journalist—the ability to *feel* the truth, despite contradictions around me; the ability to *read* people and situations accurately; the ability to be at the right place at the right time. Not long ago, I reflected upon these abilities and began to see a pattern.

Yes, we report the facts, but we are often led to them by our *instincts*. As a journalist I'm always operating within a paradoxical blend of skepticism and blind faith. I'm skeptical of everything I see and hear, but I have faith in what I *feel*. Like most everyone else, I always took credit for my highly developed intuition, my instincts, my gut reactions. *I'm so smart*, I thought. I was well into my thirties before I realized the obvious—those aren't things I can take credit for, they're part of a guidance system provided by the universe. It's Fate. Or God. Or His messengers, the angels. Whatever you label it. *I'm* not generating the information or the circumstances, I'm simply *receiving* it from elsewhere.

Viewing these instincts and events from that perspective I was amazed at just how much guidance I'd been receiving my whole life. And how well things would turn out when I listened to it. And how awful when I didn't. Even when I didn't listen to the instinctive voice, and things took a messy turn, something good or instructive would eventually come out of it. I think this is the way that we end up back on course. We're a bit the worse for wear, but we get where we're supposed to go.

Sometimes the messages are so powerful that we absolutely *must* listen to them and follow them. And we're quite happy that we did because we're alive to talk about it.

✳

In the spring of 1974, my best friend, Anne, and I were eighteen-year-old high-school seniors about to graduate. In the fall we'd be going off to attend a large university some five hundred miles from the suburban town we lived in, along with a few of our other friends. Anne decided not to bring her car with her. Like most teenagers' first cars, hers was secondhand, long on personality but short on reliability. And besides, she figured, she'd be living on campus and wouldn't really need it.

The night before the car's new owner was supposed to pick it up at Anne's home, we decided to bid farewell to the old beige four-door by taking it on one last adventure. We'd have dinner at a great barbecue place we'd been to before, in another suburb about twenty miles away. Going around the block for chicken, ribs, and fries just wouldn't do. We wanted to *drive*. It would take us thirty minutes each way at least, and there was the added bonus of the expressway. New exits near the restaurant had been added and we wanted to check that out, too.

Anne picked me up at 5:00 P.M. and the drive down was uneventful. We reminisced about all the times the car had been in the shop all year. About the mechanic whom Anne now considered to be almost part of the family.

After dinner, we drove around town for a while. Anne was feeling sentimental.

"That was the last time I'll drive this car out of a restaurant parking lot," Anne sighed, as if she were saying good-bye to the great love of her life. "And it was the last time I'll turn on the ignition."

We laughed and continued the "last times" until the sun began to go down. It was nearly 8:00 and not quite dark when we began hunting for the new expressway on-ramp. We couldn't find it. We saw the expressway, but every road we tried didn't lead us to it. We didn't see any signs, so we kept circling, trying one little side street after another.

"Up ahead on the right," I said pointing. "Maybe that's it."

As we got closer we knew we'd finally found it. The on-ramp became an overpass, and though trees blocked our view, we could tell that eventually it led to the highway.

The deep charcoal-gray sky was streaked with orange and pink at the horizon. Fluffy clouds hung overhead. The cars on the highway were beginning to turn their headlights on. Anne hadn't turned ours on yet.

I had an eerie feeling as we drove up the on-ramp. Where were the familiar green-and-white signs? Gaining speed so we'd eventually merge into the traffic at fifty-five miles per hour, Anne zoomed up the incline. Since the on-ramp doubled as an overpass we couldn't see what was on the down side, as the ramp merged into the right lane of the expressway. We could only see what was between us and the crest of the ramp. Anne was already going forty-five miles per hour.

Suddenly, in my mind I saw a cliff. I saw that the road abruptly ended just beyond the crest. That the on-ramp's construction had not been completed. That it didn't *have* a down side that led into traffic.

"Anne!" I screamed. "Stop the car! It's a cliff! Stop the car!"

Ann didn't see a cliff, and looking out the window, neither did I. We both could only see the road rising toward the crest. But I *knew* the cliff was there. I saw it in my mind. I *felt* it.

"It's a cliff!" I screamed again. "Stop the car!"

Anne didn't say a word. She hit the brakes, and the car spun around as it came to a stop just before the crest. We were fine. We got out of the car and walked up toward the crest. There were no signs, no lights, no barricades. And no road. It did stop, just as I'd seen it in my mind. Just the other side of the crest the on-ramp simply stopped. With at least a thirty-foot drop to the highway below.

We stood there in amazement.

"How could they do this?" I said, aghast at the bureaucratic stupidity that had left an unfinished overpass without warning, a death-drop just waiting for unsuspecting drivers like us.

Anne was speechless. She didn't bother asking me how I knew that the cliff was there, just moments before we would have plunged right over it. She knew that although I hadn't seen it with my eyes, I'd seen it nonetheless. She knew me well enough, and had known me long enough to have witnessed plenty of other occasions when my intuition was in high gear.

The next morning, while Anne was exchanging her car for a cashier's check, I was walking, having a little chat with God. I knew that morning that the strong intuitive powers that I'd had all my life were a gift. They were a spiritual partnership, I see now. My guardian angel showed me, in my mind, that a cliff awaited us, not twenty feet from where Anne's car eventually came to a halt. I trusted what I saw in my mind, and so did Anne. I know now that what we were trusting was a spiritual guidance that intervened to save our lives.

I went to college some five hundred miles away from home, and would visit my family twice a year for a week or two. It was January 1980, and after having taken a few years off to work in various media-related positions, I returned full-time to the university. I had just been home for a holiday visit with my family and while there spent time with my eighty-five-year-old grandfather, who had recently been moved to a nursing home. Between his heart and cancer, we knew he would not live much longer.

That January morning I had a nine o'clock class, then another at ten o'clock across campus. When I got out of the first class, I walked to my car with every intention of going to the next one. But once I started the car, I had the sense that I shouldn't go to class. This wasn't the usual "let's skip that class" feeling that students succumb to. I had an urgent feeling about this.

Something told me not only that I shouldn't go to this class, but that I shouldn't go anywhere else either, except back to my apartment.

"Well, okay," I thought. "I'll just go home."

I just *knew* it was the right thing to do, regardless of what I might be missing in class. I tossed all guilt aside and drove back to my apartment. I walked in the door and before I could even set my purse down, the phone rang.

"This must be why I had to come home," I thought. "To be here for this phone call."

I picked up the phone and knew I had made the right choice as soon as I heard my mother's voice. My grandfather had died that morning, she said.

"Pack right away," she told me, "and go to the airport. We've arranged for a ticket for you."

The funeral would be held the next morning in a city fifteen hundred miles away and I had to get on the next plane.

Once again, the little voice, the sense that I followed, had led me in the right direction.

The universe and its angels are especially sensitive to our needs and our safety when we travel. It's no coincidence that so many stories of angelic assistance revolve around cars, planes, and trains. If this were 150 years ago we'd be hearing about close calls on horseback, and "that time I just *knew* I shouldn't take that particular stagecoach."

When we travel we're especially vulnerable to all sorts of danger, mishaps, and confusion. Not to mention the logistics involved. Here's where angels can do their finest, most memorable, and often most amusing work. We've seen how "seeing in her mind" that a road turned into a cliff had been a blessing for Leigh and how following her instincts had saved her and her friend Anne from driving the car into oblivion. Now, meet Kate, thirty-eight, who saw the lighter side of travelers' assistance, angel style. She tells us in her own words about an amusing episode that happened fourteen years ago.

I had flown to Connecticut to attend a family celebration, and arrived with two small suitcases filled with sweaters and other assorted winter clothes that take up so much space. I'd be staying for three days there, then going on to Philadelphia to visit with friends for another three days.

Every time I went to Connecticut, my favorite aunt and I always went shopping together, so when my visit was over and she was taking me to the airport, I was leaving with *four* suitcases. My friend Caroline would be picking me up at the Philadelphia airport, but I'd have to wait more than an hour for her, since she'd be swinging by after work.

"How are you going to carry four suitcases from the luggage carousel to where she's picking you up?" my aunt asked. It hadn't occurred to her that that's what skycaps are for, but then again, it hadn't occurred to *me* either.

"Oh, don't worry," I replied, genuinely unconcerned. "Some nice lumberjack will carry them for me."

I checked my baggage and boarded the plane.

As the engines roared, one last passenger came sprinting down the aisle looking for his assigned seat.

The seat next to me was empty, and it matched the row number and seat letter on the man's boarding pass. I watched as he placed his overnight bag in the compartment above us. He was thirtyish, about six-foot-five, solidly built, and had sandy brown hair with a matching close-cropped beard. He wore a red, blue, and green plaid flannel shirt, blue jeans, and sturdy camel-colored work boots.

This was one rugged guy, and in fact, he was a dead ringer for the giant in the Hungry Jack pancake commercials.

He sat down next to me, out of breath.

"I can't believe I almost missed the plane," he said. He had a kind manner and gentle, almost serene face for one who was so rugged. "So, are you going to see family in Philadelphia?"

"No, I'm visiting friends there," I replied.

"Me, too," he said. "What kind of work do you do?"

"I'm a writer," I said. "How 'bout you?"

"I'm a lumberjack," he said.

My mouth opened wide, but it made no sounds. In my head, though, I screamed: *"You're a LUMBERJACK?"* How many lumberjacks can there actually be left on the planet? I'd never met one. No one I know had ever met one. Have you ever met one? I didn't think so. I couldn't believe that not fifteen minutes after jokingly telling my aunt not to worry, that a nice lumberjack would carry my suitcases, here I was sitting next to a nice lumberjack who would, in all probability, end up carrying my suitcases.

If he noticed the intense shock on my face, he didn't let on. For the rest of the flight, which was little more than a half-hour, we rarely spoke. Just a bit of small talk here and there. Mostly we both read magazines. Thoughts were racing through my mind: What were the odds of this lumberjack showing up like this? What was he doing in Connecticut, on his way to Philadelphia, when the place you'd most likely find a lumberjack would be in the Northwest, like Washington state or Oregon where there's a logging industry? What was going on here?

I never mentioned to him the comment I'd made to my aunt, or that I had four suitcases and only two arms. I never asked for help.

The plane landed, and although he only had the overnight bag he'd carried onto the plane, he followed me to the luggage carousel. My four suitcases came sliding down right away. He said he didn't have any luggage coming.

"Would you like help carrying your suitcases?" he asked.

"Yes, thanks," I answered, expecting that he'd carry two and I'd carry two.

He scooped up all four of them, holding one under each arm, and one in each hand, with his bag slung over his shoulder. I carried my purse and we walked side by side.

"Where's your friend picking you up?" he asked.

I told him, apologizing for it being clear across the airport.

"I don't mind," he said. "It's no problem."

Again, we hardly spoke. We walked and walked, then he plopped my suitcases down gently, all four at once it seemed, right in front of one of those curved, plastic airport waiting area chairs.

"Thank you so much," I said. "I really appreciate it." I bent down to line my suitcases up. I intended to stand back up and shake his hand. But when I returned to an upright position he had vanished into the crowd. It all happened very quickly. I looked around and he was simply gone. At six-five he should have been easy to spot, towering over everyone around him. But I didn't see him anywhere.

I remembered that ancient phrase: "Ask and ye shall receive." It seemed pretty obvious to me that I'd asked for a lumberjack and had, indeed, received.

In the following story, you'll meet Maggie, a writer like many others who follow their instincts, their angelic guidance.

Maggie writes for national magazines now, primarily covering the arts, sciences, and medical research. In this story she tells us how the angels paved the way for her when she began writing full-time more than a dozen years ago.

✳

We often wonder if our guardian angels are with us all the time. It spoils our notion of privacy when we consider that their constant presence means that they're with us when we're in the bathroom. But it's not that they're going to point and laugh. They're in the bathroom for a reason. I know that from experience.

When I was in my mid-twenties, I was working in the small city where I'd gone to a large university. I'd been gathering a variety of media experience but knew that what I ultimately wanted was to write full-time.

I had flown back to my hometown to attend my brother's wedding, and on the first of my three days there, my parents were hosting a dinner at their home for more than thirty family members and friends. After my third glass of iced tea, it was time to head for the bathroom. With so many people around, I wasn't surprised to find the downstairs guest bathroom occupied. Since iced tea waits for no man, or woman, I walked upstairs to the bathroom in my parents' bedroom.

I closed the door, sat down, and glanced at the wicker basket filled with magazines. I come from a family of readers. We'll read *anywhere.* If we could waterproof it, we'd read it in the shower. One of the little joys of my childhood was getting to read what other people had on *their* coffee tables, in *their* baskets when we went visiting. So I was quite happy that I had this overflowing collection of recent magazines right at my feet. The top one caught my eye right away. It was the local city magazine. Since I hadn't lived there in eight years, I'd never seen it but had heard that it was one of the finest in the country. What a treat—my parents were subscribers and not only did they have the current issue right on top, but there were plenty of back issues buried in the stack.

I flipped through the current issue and immediately knew

that I would write for them. Knew deep inside that *that's* where I belonged. I flipped back to the first few pages and looked to see if I knew anyone in the staff listing. Nope, not one person. It didn't matter. I had the most certain sensation that it was my destiny.

I left the bathroom with a major life and career decision made. I was moving back. And I was going to write for them. I didn't say anything to my family until after the wedding. As soon as I walked into my apartment three days later, after flying back, I called them.

"I'm ready to leave here," I announced. "I've done all I can here; it's time for me to take the plunge and be a full-time writer. And the most logical place for me to begin is in my hometown, a big city I know well, with lots of opportunities."

They thought I was crazy.

"Do you have a job lined up?" my parents asked.

"I will when I get there," I replied, explaining about the bathroom, the magazine, and my gut feeling. "Everything will fall into place, you'll see."

They continued to think I was crazy.

"Can you just walk in off the street and say, *Hi, I'm your new writer?*" they asked, feeling certain that the answer was no.

"That's exactly what I intend to do," I replied with the kind of confidence that comes with these instinctive feelings. "But not with those words necessarily."

"Don't you need some kind of introduction to the editor? I thought it was hard to break in. Isn't there some official way you're supposed to do this?" my mother inquired.

"Oh, of course, there are plenty of rules," I responded. "So naturally I intend to break each and every one of them, because nobody ever got anywhere by playing by the book. They say you're never supposed to call an editor if you don't know him or her. Editors are busy people who don't have the time or the inclination to talk to you. Well, I'm going to call her, and I know she's going to see me. And I'm going to give her my résumé, show her the handful of articles I've already had published, and pitch some story ideas to her. And when I leave, I'm going to have an assignment."

"How can you be so sure?" my father asked, with his usual skepticism.

"I don't know. But I'm sure," I said, trying to show him that I wasn't some cocky young woman, but one who just felt that this was destiny and it was going to come very easily. "I can't explain it any other way."

"Where will you live?" my father asked, hoping to trip me up on that little detail, too.

"I've already taken care of that," I said. "I'm going to move in with Jenny." We had been friends since high school, roommates on and off during college and after, and she'd moved back to the city about a year earlier. I planned to live with her for a while until I settled in, and then get my own place. Years earlier, she'd once shown up on my doorstep at 2:00 A.M. after finally having had enough of a perfectly wretched roommate the university had assigned her. I made room for her and she lived with me for the remainder of the semester, so I figured my moving in with her now would make us even.

"When are you moving?" my mother asked, expecting that this was some long-range plan.

"Well, let's see," I said. "Today is Tuesday. It'll take me a few days to clear things up here. I'll be there Friday night."

Again, they thought I was crazy.

But I didn't have a lease to worry about. That was in my roommate's name, and she had a friend who could take my place. I would give away or sell everything that wouldn't fit into my little car—it was time to get rid of the college-era stuff that passed for furniture anyway—nestle my cat into the front seat, and go. It would be easy. Everything would fall into place. I just *knew* it. The universe would pave the way for me. I didn't have one drop of doubt and wasn't dissuaded by anyone else's doubts either.

Well, the angels must've been working overtime because everything did fall into place effortlessly. When I arrived well after midnight on Friday—okay, it wasn't entirely smooth sailing, it rained the whole way, turning an eight-hour trip into a twelve-hour one, but I didn't care—I knew I had made the right decision, the only decision I *could* have made.

On Monday, I called the editor and asked to make an appointment. She would be happy to see me, she said, and when she learned of my media background, there was an instant kinship—she had previously been a newspaper television critic and was very pleased to have another writer on board who could cover the media.

When we met four days later, it was like the reunion of two old friends. She gave me an assignment right on the spot. The idea I pitched her just happened to be something she'd been wanting for a long time, but she hadn't found someone with the right experience to write it—until I walked in out of nowhere. As it turned out, my brother had gone to high school with hers, and my editor and I had gone to the same university, although she was about six years ahead of me. We had friends in common, too.

That first assignment turned out to be a cover story and was nominated for a journalism award. I didn't win, but it didn't matter. My editor ended up as close to me as family. She introduced me to the man I would marry. I ended up divorcing him, but I didn't hold that against her! My work for that magazine led me to write for others around the country, and ultimately for some of the biggest national magazines as well.

In short, my little trip to the bathroom ended up changing my life, launching my writing career, and opening amazing professional and personal doors. I know I was guided to take that leap. So, yes, angels do tag along when you go to the bathroom. But they won't flush for you.

You'll remember Gordon MacRae as the star of movie musicals in the fifties, such classics as *Oklahoma!* and *Carousel*. The late actor's wife, Sheila MacRae, starred with Gordon on stage, screen, and television and is best remembered as Jackie Gleason's TV wife, Alice Kramden, who put up with Gleason's gruff but ultimately lovable bus driver, Ralph Kramden, in *The Honeymooners* from 1967 to 1973, then continued her career in Broadway plays and touring companies.

Sheila MacRae now divides her time between homes in California and New York, and often speaks publicly about the spiritual experiences she's had throughout her childhood and adult life.

Over the years, Sheila has told me about the many instances when her intuition, her angel guidance, has both delighted her and warned her of danger. She chose these stories to share with you.

Back in 1946, before their Hollywood successes, Sheila and Gordon were a young married couple not unlike many others of their time. Gordon was in the Army Air Corps (which would become the Air Force, a separate military branch), stationed in Texas, where he was training pilots. Sheila was pregnant, and the couple eagerly awaited the birth of their child as Gordon spent long days away from his wife in flight maneuvers.

One day, around Thanksgiving, at about eleven in the morning, Sheila "jumped up, knowing something was wrong with Gordy," she remembers. "I couldn't call him because he was in training exercises all day and couldn't be reached by phone."

The feeling that came over her was so intense she couldn't ignore it. It wouldn't pass, and she felt helpless. She knew she had to do *something*.

"Pray," suggested her landlady.

Sheila prayed. She began reciting the Ninety-first Psalm,

well known for its theme of God's protection and its references
to angels:

> For he shall give his angels charge over thee, to keep thee in
> all thy ways.
> They shall bear thee up in their hands, lest thou dash thy foot
> against a stone.
> Thou shalt tread upon the lion and adder: the young lion and
> the dragon shalt thou trample under feet.
> Because he hath set his love upon me, therefore will I deliver
> him: I will set him on high, because he hath known my
> name.
> He shall call upon me, and I will answer him: I will be with
> him in trouble; I will deliver him, and honour him.
> With long life will I satisfy him, and shew him my salvation.

Sheila recited the entire Psalm and prayed for her husband's
safety. She didn't know the nature of the danger he was in, but
she felt, deep in her soul, that Gordon was in trouble.

She prayed and she prayed and she prayed.

Finally, at 6:00 P.M., he phoned from the base.

"You'll never believe this," Gordon said to his wife on the
phone. "We were in the air and the copilot panicked and froze
at the controls. They said we'd have to jump!"

"What time was this?" Sheila asked, relieved to hear her husband's voice, and not at all surprised that something so dramatic
had happened.

"Around eleven this morning," Gordon replied.

Eleven that morning—the same time that Sheila had sensed
Gordon in danger.

"Suddenly I heard this voice saying the Ninety-first Psalm,"
Gordon continued. "And I unlocked the copilot's hands and
landed the plane myself. It's a good thing I didn't jump. One of
the guys who did died because we were flying so low."

Gordon had heard Sheila's prayer. He didn't jump, he didn't

panic. Feeling divine protection, he was able to take over and help land the plane, saving their lives.

Some time later, Sheila's spiritual guidance helped save her husband once again. Sheila and their baby were living on Long Island, New York, while Gordon was stationed at Pope Field in North Carolina. On Fridays, Gordon would fly to New York to spend the weekend with his wife and family. One week, though, Sheila sensed that Gordon should *not* fly to Roosevelt Field in Long Island, New York, that she, instead, should travel to North Carolina to be with him for the weekend.

Her family tried to talk her out of it.

"It's such a long trip to make," they protested. "And you have the baby. Stay here. He'll fly up on Friday. What's the difference?"

There *was* a difference. Sheila didn't know exactly what it *was*, but she knew that she could not let Gordon come to New York that Friday. Her mind was made up and no one could talk her out of it. The travel plans were tricky, and she ended up making a long train trip from New York south to North Carolina. Shortly after her arrival on Friday, she and Gordon were at a party at a colonel's home, when an officer suddenly burst into the room.

"I got a chill when I saw him," Sheila remembers. "I watched him go over and speak quietly with the colonel, then the colonel called Gordon over."

After speaking with his superior, Gordon walked back to Sheila.

"I've got to go to New York," he told her. "Everyone on the plane to Roosevelt Field was killed."

Preparing to land in heavy fog, the plane hit a tree and crashed.

That was the plane that Gordon would have been on.

✳

By 1953, Sheila and Gordon were enjoying fame and a comfortable lifestyle in Hollywood. With a growing family (they eventually had four children), the couple began looking to buy a bigger home. A real estate agent took Sheila out to see a beautiful ranch house that also had a pool, walnut groves, a barn, and a corral filled with horses.

"I loved it," Sheila says. "It was perfect for a big family. But when I stepped up to walk into the house, I felt faint. 'I can't live in this house,' I said to the real estate agent and the man who owned it."

"Don't be silly," the owner replied. "You just don't feel well because you're pregnant. Come in and have some milk and crackers."

Sheila didn't want to enter the house, but she followed them in. The owner's wife wasn't feeling well, and was lying down, he told them, so he'd go into the kitchen and prepare the milk and crackers for Sheila.

"I knew I had to get out of there," Sheila says. "But he wanted me to stay. He went for the milk, telling me that he wanted to take us outside afterward and show us the horses. A few of them would be included in the sale."

Feeling uneasy, Sheila walked toward the kitchen.

"I saw a breakfast nook," she remembers. "And then a vision materialized in it. Through a grayish-white haze I saw a woman sitting at the table smoking a cigarette. As soon as I saw that, I felt so ill, I told them, 'I've got to get out of here!' "

Sheila ran out of the house immediately. It was 5:00 P.M.

In the car, driving home, the real estate woman kept saying to Sheila, "You should've stayed. You should have seen the rest of the house!"

But Sheila was relieved to be out of there.

As soon as she got home, Sheila felt better.

"I can't live in that house," she said to Gordon. She told him of the vision she had seen in the breakfast nook.

"Oh, it was probably just shadows," he replied.

But Sheila knew better.

At 9:00 P.M. their phone rang.

"It was the real estate woman," Sheila recalls. "She called to tell us that the big, beautiful home I'd seen that afternoon had burned down. The wife was an alcoholic, and her cigarette caused the fire."

The vision Sheila had—of a woman smoking a cigarette in the breakfast nook, surrounded by a smoky haze—and the terrible fear that made her run from the house was a message.

"I *saw* it before it happened."

By 1966, Sheila was starring as Alice in the updated *Honeymooners*, which she would continue on CBS until 1970.

"Jackie would always test me," she recalls, "and we'd have discussions about ESP and guardian angels."

That first year she joined the show (which had already been running for four years), she received another spiritual message about an airplane, but this time it involved her dear friend Frank Sinatra.

"I woke up at 5:00 A.M. from a dream," she remembers. "And all I could think of was that Frank shouldn't go on his plane. I was in New York, and it was 2:00 A.M. in Palm Springs, where Frank was, but I kept thinking, 'I have to call him!' "

"Don't fly today," she told Frank on the phone.

"As a matter of fact, Dean and I are flying to San Diego today," Frank told her, referring to Dean Martin.

"Don't go!" she implored.

"Don't be silly," he said, trying to comfort her. "It's only a short hop."

Frank took the flight and phoned Sheila later in the day.

"Hello, Mrs. Witch," he said, teasing her when she answered

the phone. "We're okay, but the plane blew a tire on landing and ran off the runway."

In 1986, Gordon MacRae died. Although he and Sheila had been divorced for some time, they had remained close friends, the spiritual bond between them as strong as it had always been.

"The night Gordon died I cried myself to sleep," she says. "And when I woke up in the morning I saw him, his spirit, lying on the other side of the bed. He was wearing his favorite green plaid pajamas. I screamed, jumped up, and ran out. I shouldn't have done that. I came back in and he was gone."

Like many who have seen the spirits of loved ones who have died, Sheila believes that Gordon appearing in her bed was a divine message to console her, and to show her that he was all right, safe and protected in the afterlife.

About the angelic assistance she has always been so aware of, Sheila has this to say: "We don't always listen. Listening is the hard part." But if you *do* listen, she believes, you'll be amazed at the information that you're given, and even more amazed at how you can play a role assisting the angels in the protection of your loved ones.

When Sheila prayed for Gordon's safety, reciting the Ninety-first Psalm, she unknowingly did what the angels love best. Angels adore praying, and they respond. I like to compare prayers to a call button or a beeper we use to summon divine assistance.

The angels like group prayer, when two or more people join in summoning their assistance. The Bible, in fact, makes many references to this phenomenon, to "two or more" praying in the name of God.

Angels have a long tradition of appearing in people's dreams. You'll remember how they appeared that way to Joseph to guide him and his family to safety after Jesus' birth. Sometimes the angels choose to appear to you in dreams because it's a comfortable way for you to receive their specific messages. When Sheila awoke from a dream knowing that Frank Sinatra shouldn't get on a plane that day, she was experiencing this common form of angelic communication.

When you dream, the angels can take you into many other dimensions, sometimes even to see people who have passed on. When you awake, you can ask the angels to help you interpret the dreams you have had, and they will.

What Can't They Do for Us?

As I mentioned before, the angels only work as a force for *good*, so they won't be your avenging army. They also won't make your life perfect. That's your job. They will protect you from harm, but if you're not listening to that feeling inside, and you ignore their warnings or suggestions, you may end up in a pickle! They can't make you listen to them. They'll try very hard, but ultimately it's up to you!

When they do their work, they're also assisting us in the life lessons we're learning. That's why they don't just provide a perfect, lovely, hassle-free life for us. If they did *that*, we would never learn anything! Think of it as school. We didn't have perfect knowledge and answers implanted in our brains. We had to read, learn, experience. And often we were tested to see how much we learned. An angel doesn't take the tests for us but *tutors* us in a very special way, providing more help than we ever dreamed possible.

ℋ︁OW DO THEY TEACH US LESSONS?

They teach us about faith, about trusting ourselves, and about the "little voice" we each have inside us. They teach us about love; about the difference between good and bad; about respecting life in all its forms.

How do they do this?

By putting us in situations where we will learn. These lessons are beautiful, but some can be painful.

Marie Marshall lives in New Port Richey, Florida, on the Gulf Coast not far from Tampa. She wrote to me after attending one of my lectures about angels, to relay this incredible story. In her own words, here's what happened.

It all started just before midnight one night. I had been reading a book about angels that I received from Linda after attending one of her lectures. I have always believed in guardian angels, but so far had never really experienced such a clear-cut, unmistakable message that the angels were at work as this one.

After losing nearly everything to Hurricane Andrew in South Florida, my son had temporarily moved in with my husband and me. Since we had stored his furnishings in our garage, we had to park our brand-new pickup truck in the driveway. Just before midnight, I had showered and retired to bed. I decided to pick up my new book on angels and read it. I couldn't wait until the next day. I had been telling my son and husband about the book earlier in the evening, and I remembered that they had both looked at me with that "let's humor her" look, and went about their business.

While I read, at midnight, my son was settled in the guest bedroom and my husband was taking a shower. I was on page twenty-five, and very absorbed in my book. I remember feeling very peaceful, and somewhere other than where I was physically located!

All at once, there was an earth-shattering loud noise, and the house shook. It sounded as if we were under attack, and our house had taken a direct hit! In an instant I was up, out of bed, and heading for the front door, where I met my son already on his way out. My husband was still in the shower, completely oblivious to what was taking place.

Together, my son and I went out to the front yard. We couldn't believe what we saw. Although there wasn't another human soul around, the area from our house and down three houses to the corner looked as if it had gone through a war.

It seems a car had made a turn to enter our street, lost control, gone off the road, and plowed through the front yards of the first three houses to the right of ours, taking the mailbox, some shrubs, and an ornament from the first house on the corner; taking the mailbox, shrubs, plants, and ornaments from the second house; and shearing two permanently cemented electrical power boxes, a small tree, and lots of dirt and grass from the third house, which was just to the right of ours. The car's tire tracks came across their driveway and were headed right on target toward our new pickup truck parked in our driveway.

It had rained earlier, which allowed us to see the clear trail of mud and dirt that the out-of-control car had made. It led right up to our property line, where the tracks mysteriously came to a sudden stop. The property frontage on each house is only thirty feet across. The car had to be going pretty fast to get as far as it did, especially after shearing off the electrical boxes!

By this time, my husband had joined my son and me. The neighbors were starting to come out and I remember all of us looking in disbelief at how the tracks came to an abrupt stop right at our property line, which would have placed the car just *two feet* from the driver's door of our new pickup truck.

We could see where the car backed up away from our truck, and turned to the right to get back on the road. Looking at the tire mark, the car should have hit the back bumper of our truck on its way back to the street, but it didn't. There was something very odd about the last six feet of tire marks. It seemed that the car hardly touched the ground, since the marks hardly showed, considering the weight of the car. It was as if something had picked the car up and held it, or stopped it in its tracks.

The only thing missing was the car and driver. I stood there in total disbelief as what happened was absorbed into my conscious mind. I turned to my son and husband and said: "*Now* do you believe in angels?"

The next day, as the power company was replacing the electrical boxes, I went outside with my camera and captured the evidence, still as visible as the night before. Another odd thing—the other three houses were without electricity for that night and the next day, until the repairs were made. Our house was not affected.

Since that night, I have become more active communicating with angels. I ask my angels for guidance with almost everything. It's like having a special friend with you all the time.

I have learned that there is an angel for everything. You can use them as you would use the yellow pages. When I'm sewing, I ask for a "designer angel" to help me. I love my angels, and I've seen them do some pretty profound work.

One day recently my husband came home and said that he had been having a difficult time helping out a neighbor. He said he remembered what I had said about angels and asked them for help. To his surprise, the problem was resolved instantly.

My son asked for angel help when he was planning his move from our house to Georgia. The first day he arrived in Georgia he landed a good job and was able to buy a house. He had absolutely no money for a down payment. Need I say more? The two skeptics have now become firm believers in "angel power" and would not dream of being without them.

The Marshalls' son and many others in South Florida experienced everything from minor inconvenience to total destruction during Hurricane Andrew.

I was out of town as the hurricane approached and when it hit. Worried about the large black olive tree in my yard, I prayed to the angels. I asked them to guide the tree if it were to be knocked down by the storm's fierce winds. I knew that there was only one place where it could fall and not hit my house or my neighbor's, only one narrow place for it to topple over where it wouldn't do any damage to any property at all. I prayed that the angels direct the falling tree to land in that one safe place.

I returned home after the hurricane came through, and sure enough my black olive tree had fallen. And it fell exactly the way I had prayed it would.

On Labor Day, 1979, Kathy, then thirty- two, was baking cookies with her three school-age children when the phone rang.

"It was my husband, Jason," she recalls. "He had gone into the woods to cut wood for our fireplace, and the chain on his chainsaw broke. He hadn't brought his extra chain with him, so he walked to one of the houses on the mountain and called me, asking me to bring him his extra chain."

Kathy hopped into their Jeep with their son, Alan, then nine.

"The roads up the mountain where we lived then in upstate New York were very curvy and dangerous," she remembers. "We were coming around a curve, and I remember I was only going forty-eight miles an hour and driving very cautiously, when suddenly the steering wheel started spinning around and around. Something in the mechanism must've snapped."

Kathy tried to control the car, but couldn't. The steering was gone.

"The next thing I remember," she continues, "I was waking up in the hospital. I learned that the Jeep had flipped three times. Alan was thrown from the Jeep. I was thrown clear across the road into a field. Some people stopped when they saw Alan running in circles in the middle of the road. He was in shock."

He didn't know where his mother was, and it wasn't until the ambulance arrived that she was found unconscious, sprawled out in the field.

"I woke up in the emergency room with a broken vertebra in my neck, a broken shoulder, and my front teeth broken," she says. "Alan needed some stitches from where he'd hit the pavement, but he was okay."

Given the severity of the crash, "everyone was surprised that we lived," she says. "When you're thrown like that, you're not supposed to live."

Kathy believes that someone or something was definitely watching over her that day, and protected her.

Why didn't she die?

"It wasn't my time yet," she believes. "Someone had to raise the kids. My husband couldn't have done it alone."

Then why did she have the accident?

"It was like a wake-up call, a kick in the pants," she says. "After waking up in the hospital that day I've never been the person I'd been before, never felt the same again. Not long after the accident, I did what I should have done years earlier. I left a marriage that could never work."

Kathy moved south and now works in real estate. She met a wonderful man whom she has been with for the last eight years. Her three children are grown, and in the spring of 1993 she became a grandmother.

She still feels the presence of her guardian angels.

Kathy is just one of millions of people each day who have close calls. In the last twenty years I have heard hundreds of these stories of angelic protection and have experienced a few of my own, some behind the wheel of a car as Kathy was.

The angels guided my hands as I drove my car when I was lost, turning the wheel left and right to get me safely where I needed to be in the middle of night. I felt their warmth as my hands rested on the steering wheel.

Ten years ago, the angels kept my foot on the brake as I sat at a light. I tried to move my foot to the accelerator when my light turned green, but my foot simply would not move. I didn't know what was wrong: Was my leg suddenly paralyzed? With my foot firmly stuck on the brake I watched as a car ran a red light and flew by right in front of me. Had I been able to move my foot I would have been in that intersection and certainly would've been hit broadside by that car. Once that car passed by me I heard a voice say, "Now you can go." And with that my foot left the brake and moved to the accelerator!

The angels once again intervened on another occasion. I was driving down the highway when a flying tire came straight at me, only to be deflected mysteriously by who knows what. It should have hit my car, but it disappeared. The angels protected me once again.

What About Free Will?

We all have free will. We have choices, and we make them. We certainly can decide, for example, to *not* ask for help, or not to accept it when it's given. And we can ignore the angels' messages. We have plenty of opportunities to take matters into our own hands.

We also have the free will to ask for help, accept it, and follow the intuitive gut feelings that are the avenue in which the angels travel with their messages.

In 1973, Laura Caster was a high-school student with a broken heart.

"I had spent most of that summer away at a special university program for advanced science students, and when I came home my boyfriend told me that he had found someone else," she remembers. "He was my first love, and he had left me."

Laura was crushed.

"I sat up in my bed and cried all night, asking over and over for help to get him back," she says.

Late in the evening, as she sat there in tears, she heard a voice, a gentle, soothing, male, almost fatherly voice.

"All right, my child," said the voice.

When she heard that, Laura calmed down and fell asleep.

The next morning the phone rang.

"I've made a terrible mistake," Laura's boyfriend told her

over the phone. "I woke up this morning and I was missing you terribly. I want to see you."

Laura couldn't believe what was happening. Her teenage prayers had been answered.

"We got back together," Laura remembers. "It didn't last very long, but at least we had that second chance."

When they did break up for good, Laura remembers she didn't feel quite as bad as the first time, and she now looks back on him fondly.

Laura was sixteen, and he was eighteen then. As Laura tells this story, twenty years have passed. She went off to college, married a man she met there, had two daughters, and is now divorced and living in upstate New York.

Whatever became of her first love?

"He married the girl he first left me for," Laura says, without a trace of bitterness. "I know it was spiritual intervention that gave us a second chance, but I guess he was destined to be with her after all."

Laura has always felt spiritual assistance around her, and she tells this story about what can happen when you don't or can't follow what the inner voice, the angelic voice, tells you.

After college, when I was married, my husband and I were living out in the country in a house just up a path from his parents' home. We had a seven-month-old registered and papered black-and-tan Doberman named Spooky. Since this was out in the country he wasn't on a chain and was free to roam all over the place.

One day, our three cats climbed out the window and up to the roof.

"We have to get them down," I said to my husband.

We walked down the path to his parents' house to get a ladder. Spooky greeted us from inside my in-laws' door. When we had what we needed, we went out the door and Spooky began following us back to our house.

"I think you should leave her here," I said, sensing danger, sensing that Spooky shouldn't be running around outside while we were on the roof.

"No, she can come along," my husband said.

"I really think we should leave her here," I said again.

He waved me off, as if to say that everything would be all right, and let the dog come with us back to our house.

While we were on the roof with the cats, Spooky got hit by a car. I never forgave myself for letting my husband talk me into letting the dog out. The car didn't kill her, but she was crippled for the rest of her life, which was only another six months. She died because her leg didn't heal.

Like Laura, we've all had indications that we should do this or do that (or not do this or that!), and when we don't listen or are prevented from following this guidance the consequences are unpleasant.

Once, I was driving behind a friend's car, and even though I heard the angelic message "Slow down! You're going to have an accident!" I continued at full speed. I should have known better. My friend's car suddenly slowed down and I was following so close to her that I hit the back of her car. Had I slowed down when I'd been told, I would have had plenty of time to keep a safe distance behind her when she slowed down.

. . .

What Are Our Responsibilities?

Remember when we were children, how our parents provided us with a home to live in, clothes to wear, food to eat? We weren't responsible for paying rent or a mortgage, and we didn't have to work in order to buy what we needed. We didn't have to shop for our clothes (until we were old enough to want to pick out things with Mom or Dad) or our food. We didn't have to cook dinner. Well, you see what I mean. At this early stage of our lives we had few responsibilities. But we did have them. We were responsible for growing and learning. We were responsible for going to school, doing our homework. When we were about two, we were responsible for becoming toilet-trained. When we were three, we were taking on more re-sponsibilities: learning how to share our toys, how to put them away when we were done playing.

As we grew we took on more and more responsibilities.

As adults we're just loaded with responsibilities! They don't change just because we are more aware of angelic assistance. What can change, though, is our *attitude* about our responsibil-ities. Perhaps we can worry less when we realize that after we've done absolutely everything we can in a situation, the rest is in the hands of the universe. Perhaps we don't worry as much about the big things and the little things when we realize we're *not* alone, that there's help and guidance available to us always, that sometimes we don't even have to ask for it.

Ron Renneberg says he saved his son's life once because he stayed home when he was supposed to go fishing.

"Something told me to stay home," he says now in Florida, nearly twenty years after the incident happened, when he and his family were living in Connecticut.

Ron, a second-generation police officer, was used to following that little voice inside. So, when it told him to stay home that Sunday, he turned down the fishing trip and settled in on the couch with the Sunday paper.

His wife was in the kitchen cutting up potatoes while talking on the phone, and their five-year-old son was in the kitchen with her, playing and chewing on a small piece of potato she had given him. It was a pleasant, homey scene until Ron's wife began yelling frantically from the kitchen.

Ron ran in and found her holding their son.

"He had already turned blue," Ron remembers. "He was choking on the potato."

Ron grabbed his son.

"Call nine-one-one!" he yelled to his wife.

She dialed while Ron turned the child over.

"This was before the Heimlich maneuver," Ron recalls. "So I whacked him on the back. It was all we knew to do in those days. But eventually the piece of potato flew out."

The little boy was rushed to the hospital and made a quick and complete recovery.

"I know we must have a guardian angel," Ron says now, "because if I'd gone out fishing, my son might not be alive today."

I always advise that when you do what Ron did—changing his mind about the fishing trip and deciding to stay at home— you should stick with your decision. Don't question it, just follow it. Even if you don't understand why at the moment you're doing it. As we saw, it became clear later why Ron actually needed to be home that Sunday and not go fishing.

We don't know what would have happened to Ron's son had Ron not been there. Just as we don't know what might happen when we don't follow our angelic guidance.

• • •

How Do We Know If a Feeling Is a Message from the Angels?

Boy, this is a tough one to answer simply. What I'd like to say is that we just *know*. Ask anyone who is open to assistance (and by that I mean they're always aware of their gut feelings, intuition, and instincts and they follow them most of the time), and they'll tell you that they just *feel* it. Most of us aren't used to calling these feelings "messages from the angels," but once you look at them that way, you'll be able to tell the difference most of the time!

As for coincidences, well, they're pretty obvious. I believe that coincidence, synchronicity, and serendipity are orchestrated by God, the universe, the angels. Whenever something like that happens, I smile, knowing that the angels are at play.

Often it's a judgment call. It's trial and error. Once you are aware, you can keep track of the times when it was angelic assistance, and the times when a feeling was simply a feeling. What can get confusing, though, is that angelic assistance isn't always something we're immediately aware of. It can take minutes, hours, days, weeks, months, or even years to see the effects or patterns. But, more often than not, we can figure it out pretty quickly.

"I have a *knowing*, and then it happens," says forty-one-year-old New York restaurateur Bill Lirio. "I smile and feel good about it."

It's been that way as far back as he can remember. Bill's inner guidance came in particularly handy twice in 1992. First, by taking a different flight than originally planned, he missed being on a plane that crashed in New York. "I just *knew* not to get on that plane," he says calmly, sensing the protection that always surrounds him. "Then, I couldn't believe that something so similar happened just a few months later."

Bill and his girlfriend decided to spend four days in Aspen, Colorado. It was June, so sightseeing, not skiing, would fill their first trip to the popular destination.

One morning they thought they'd like to venture up the mountains. They had a choice: either drive part of the way up and take a tram the rest of the way to the peak, or drive up and bicycle back down from a different peak.

A feeling told Bill to choose the bicycle ride.

"I'd never been in mountains like this before," he recalls. "As we were going up the mountain, the young instructor driving the truck was telling us about avalanches, explaining all these fallen trees we saw."

"Every year we have them," the instructor said. "But don't worry, we don't have avalanches at this time of year."

Bill was certainly relieved to hear *that*, but he would feel even more relieved hours later when, after an invigorating bike ride down the mountain, he and his girlfriend returned to their hotel around 6:00 P.M. to discover that they had, indeed, made the right choice.

"We found out that while we were on the bicycle trip, a rare avalanche got the people who got off the tram on the *other* trip at the peak of the other mountain," he recalls. "Two people were killed and more than a dozen were injured."

Once again, Bill remembered what he heard upon meeting a spiritual acquaintance some fifteen years earlier. "She took one look at me and said I had four angels on either side of me."

How lucky Bill is that he follows his divine guidance and lets angel power work for him! Bill already had tickets for that flight that ultimately crashed. Even with tickets in hand, he *knew* he should change his flight, and he did.

Then he followed those same instincts when he chose which Aspen sightseeing trip to take.

ARE INTUITION AND ANGELIC MESSAGES THE SAME THINGS?

I say yes. So do many other people. Even those of us who have an intense intuition we call psychic ability believe that it is a *gift*, and as such is angelic assistance.

"We each have our own kind of heaven," the angels tell Andrea, who says, "My grandmother loved flowers, so her heaven is a beautiful garden."

Andrea is a remarkable twelve-year-old girl who lives in a midwestern city with her mother, a former flight attendant, and her father, a retail manager. She's the fourth of five children, a brilliant student with many friends, and she talks to the angels.

Andrea's childhood was stable and loving, and by all accounts pretty similar to that of any outgoing, inquisitive little girl, except for a few mystical moments here and there when, out of the blue, she'd exhibit some extraordinary abilities.

"When she was three," says her mother, "one day she just started talking about another life she'd had before she was born. It seemed a bit odd to us, but we just listened, and it all seemed so natural to her."

Not long after, her mother noticed that Andrea's intuition was becoming more highly developed.

"She'd just *know* things," she says.

None of these memories or abilities played a major role in

Andrea's life, and neither she nor her family made much of them, or researched them. They neither encouraged nor discouraged them.

But it became impossible to think of Andrea as just an ordinary girl after March 1993.

"She was getting ready for school, and she called to me," her mother remembers.

"Mo Mo wants to know why you never told her any of your problems," Andrea asked her mother.

Her mother was stunned. Mo Mo was Andrea's grandmother, who had recently died.

"I didn't want to upset her," Andrea's mother replied. "What do you mean *'Mo Mo wants to know'*?"

What Andrea told her mother was nothing short of amazing.

"She was here, sitting on my bed, and she asked me to ask you," Andrea said very plainly.

"It was true that I had kept little things from my mother that I would ordinarily have told her," says Andrea's mother. "But she was so ill. Long before she died we made a pact that whichever one of us died first, we would try to contact the other from beyond, but we never told anyone about that. When she died, I wondered whether I'd see signs or feel her presence. She came through Andrea because I guess Andrea is one of those gifted people with a receptive soul."

Andrea wasn't alarmed that the spirit of her grandmother came to visit her.

"It felt very natural," says Andrea. "It didn't upset me at all."

The only thing that upsets Andrea about her gift is that she's afraid that people might think *she* thinks she's special or better than they are, and she certainly holds no holier-than-thou or snobbish attitudes about her abilities, says her mother.

"You know how kids are at this age," says Andrea's mother. "They're very concerned about how people view them."

Once Andrea's grandmother "came through," the floodgates

opened, and other souls who had passed on contacted Andrea. She didn't channel them, she simply became aware of their presence, and in her mind could communicate with them, not unlike the way we talk to ourselves silently, only Andrea got answers. Plenty of answers. Her family tested her, and Andrea passed with flying colors. She was receiving information she'd have no other way of knowing.

Not long after her grandmother's first "visit," Andrea also showed the ability to communicate directly with her guardian angels, and those of anyone else that might be requested. Information came pouring in, but the angels specifically reminded Andrea that there is much we aren't meant to know while we live.

"I could ask any questions I wanted, and the angels answered," says Andrea, just as if she were casually discussing an afternoon at school. "And they'd volunteer information, too."

Andrea and her family would hold get-togethers with the angels, privately, just the family.

"We couldn't believe at first that this was happening to us," says Andrea's mother. "I mean, we're really just an average family. We're Presbyterians, but not religious, so to speak. We don't go to church. But we believe in God, and raised our kids to believe."

The angels have told Andrea about heaven, among other things.

"Heaven is everyone's individual idea of heaven, and in the first level of heaven you stay until you're reborn. The second level of heaven is where you go if you won't be reborn. It's the eternity level," says Andrea, revealing what the angels told her. "There are spirits everywhere, spirits of those who have died. But they must not be confused with the angels. Angels have never been mortal. Our guardian angels are specially picked by God to be our guardians and teachers."

"The angels and spirits are interested in Andrea," says her mother. "They say she was chosen to pass on information, so she can help people."

She's doing that very quietly and privately. This is the first time that Andrea and her mother have spoken publicly about Andrea's gift. And they have asked that only Andrea's first name be used.

"We don't want to exploit her," says her mother. "And certainly Andrea wants to handle her gift with great dignity, too."

What's the most important thing she's learned from the angels?

"You have to be open to them, or they really can't help you," says Andrea. "If we ignore or block out our gut feelings or our better instincts, that's exactly the same thing as keeping the angels out because those thoughts and feelings we get are messages from them."

Angels enjoy presenting us with information. They'll give us what we need to know about the past, the present, and even the future, as we see in Andrea's story. And they also love acting as our receptionists, making contacts for us with people, other angels, and spirits.

THE GIFT OF DISCERNMENT

You're either born with it, or you work to develop it. If you are developing it, you will eventually be able to discern, to *know*, the difference between wishful thinking and imagination, and intuition and angelic assistance.

Trust it, go with it, and you'll *know*. You will have the truth. Of course, no one is 100 percent accurate all the time. There are always strange twists in the road! It's like being on a rollercoaster and holding on. Sometimes God wants to surprise us!

When I'm not sure if what I'm feeling is angelic assistance or an angelic message, I'll actually ask, "Who is it?"

INTUITION

Intuition is the divine force within, from the God force through an angel, spirit, saint, or just directly to you.

SYNCHRONICITY

The angels at play, orchestrating our lives—that's how I look at coincidence or its more intense variety, synchronicity.

LESSONS

We must thank God for our problems so that He will show us what we have to learn. Then we can go through it, learn it, and move on!

MEDITATION AND LISTENING

These are direct intuitive transcendental teaching processes. We clear our minds, open them up, and then *listen* to what comes in.

DO YOU HAVE TO BELIEVE IN OR PRACTICE ORGANIZED RELIGION TO BELIEVE IN ANGELS OR RECEIVE THEIR ASSISTANCE?

No, you do *not* have to be a card-carrying member of any organized (or disorganized) religion to believe in divine assistance and benefit from it.

People from all cultures are part of the dance with the universe, the divine. Native Americans have a faith that focuses on nature, Christians believe that Jesus is the Messiah, Jews believe in the same one-God principle but are still waiting for a Messiah, those of the Eastern faiths have their own unique beliefs, and the list goes on. But common to every religion or faith is some kind of divine guidance and protection.

You can still feel a connection with the divine *without* practicing Christianity, Judaism, Buddhism, or any other religion. You can believe in a force you call God, or believe in some universal power that has another name, or names, or no labels at all.

You can think of this all as one giant question mark, and not be sure if you believe in a so-called God force.

All it takes is *faith*, any kind of faith, to be in tune with the divine. Faith in mother nature, faith in yourself, faith in the workings of the universe. Maybe you're even a little rocky on the issue of faith, you're not sure you even have any. Not to worry. You still have your intuition to guide you, whether you call it angelic assistance or not. You still have plenty of coincidences to assist you, whether you believe they're orchestrated by the divine or not. The dance goes on, no matter what your perspective on it.

How Does Faith Differ from Religious and Cultural Practices, Traditions, and Doctrines?

The *Merriam-Webster Dictionary* defines faith as a belief and trust in God, as confidence, and as loyalty. The word is also used interchangeably with the word *religion*, as in, "She is of the Hindu faith." But faith and religion are two very different things. Faith is the *belief*, the *trust*. Religion is the particular *practice* you subscribe to or follow. The dictionary calls it the organized *system* of faith and worship.

You have faith. You participate or believe in a certain religious system, such as Christianity, Judaism, or Islam (or any of a number of others). Or perhaps you have faith, but don't follow a particular religion at all.

Part Four

COMMUNICATING WITH ANGELS

God is not a cosmic bellboy for whom we can press a button to get things.

—HARRY EMERSON FOSDICK, *PRAYER*

 OW DO YOU COMMUNICATE
with angels? Easily, naturally, while you sleep, and when you're
awake. When you try, and when it's not on your mind at all.

But, as you'll see in the angel experience tales that follow,
angels orchestrate events for our higher good, and while they
can certainly be called upon in just about any situation, we may
be surprised at their response!

In Part Three, we saw that angel awareness is the first step
in recognizing divine assistance. Now, in Part Four, we see that
this awareness is the key to angel communication.

How Do I Ask for Angelic Assistance?

How about "*Help*!!" That usually works.

You can think it lightly, you can concentrate on it intensely.
You can say it out loud. You can shout it from the rooftops.

It can be an offhand comment or a direct request. The angels hear both.

Being open to their assistance is the key. Learning to recognize their answers, which come most often in the form of their assistance or your gut feelings, is just as important.

You don't have to go through any ceremonies, or do anything formal, though you may do so if you like. If you aren't used to following your instincts, it may help for you to follow some of the guidelines I offer. They'll help increase your awareness.

COMMUNICATION IS AWARENESS

1. Be aware that you have access to your angels, and to angels in general, at all times.
2. Be aware that you can speak to them out loud, or speak to them in your mind. Either way, they will hear you.
3. Be aware that you must be specific about your requests. Angels take things very literally sometimes. Make things very clear to them. By doing this, you will also clarify things for yourself.
4. Be aware that you should always give thanks for the angels' eternal and continuous help. After all, it's the polite thing to do!
5. Be aware of your reactions: that means thinking positively and having faith that the angels will help you.
6. Be aware of your state of mind: Have a sense of humor. The angels certainly do. It helps, even though it may be difficult during times of tragedy to find something to chuckle about.
7. Be aware of your gut feelings, instincts, and intuition: Those are your angels talking to you!
8. Be aware of coincidence, synchronicity, serendipity, and irony: Those are also brought about by the angels!

9. Be aware of your openness. Be open intellectually, emotionally, and spiritually to the little voice that tells you things, to your instincts, to the inner guidance system that is the angels. Angels can't help you if you've shut them out.
10. Be aware of the messages. Listen, notice, learn! You'll begin to see patterns and guidance in your life. You'll gain trust in yourself and therefore in your angelic guidance.

NATURAL COMMUNICATION

All you have to do is think about the angels. They're always watching and listening. Just open your mind to them. Become aware of your instincts, intuition, and gut feelings. They are the angels talking to you!

There are two phases to angel communication: active and passive.

In the active phase we ask and pray.

In the passive phase we relax and let them work through us; we receive and absorb their energy.

If you're looking for visions and lights, forget it. Probably 90 percent of the time the angels don't *appear* with fanfare, or without! They just make things work, synchronize events, bring people into your life, protect you, and address fears and problems as well as positive situations.

Everyone has at least one thing (and probably twenty!) each day that happens, whether we are aware enough to notice it or not, that is the work of the angels. It's easy to be aware. Stop now and think about what happened today. See? You've probably come up with a pretty long list already. From now on you have awareness. It's really *that easy.*

---

*C*ONTACTING THE ANGELS

At times we feel the need to set aside a few moments to call upon our angels and have a chat. You may want to follow these steps:

1. *Make yourself physically comfortable*: Wear loose-fitting clothes, take your shoes off. Sit or lie down in a comfy setting.
2. *Remove all distractions*: noise, people, pets, phone, television.
3. *Choose your sounds*: soothing music, wind chimes, or silence.
4. *Breathe*: Take a few deep breaths to relax. Breathe slowly. Inhale positive feelings and light, exhale the negative.
5. *Seek God first*: Praise Him and thank Him for all things.
6. *Lighten up*: You don't have to be solemn, just relaxed.
7. *Go over your list of things you need assistance with*: Assign an angel to each and thank them ahead of time.
8. *Create an angel altar*: Fill a special space—top of a bureau, corner of a room—with things that remind you of the angels, such as ornaments, pins, cards, angel pictures, and other accessories. You can also add incense.

WHAT NOT TO DO

Always keep these points in mind when thinking of the angels:

1. The angels don't want you to think that they'll do all the work *for* you, because they *won't*. This is a partnership. They'll do plenty, but you'll have to do your part as well. With their guidance, you'll instinctively know what your part *is*!
2. Don't have a negative attitude or focus on greed, rage, or hatred.
3. Don't ask for revenge.
4. Don't worship the angels. They are not God. They do not want to be worshiped, just appreciated!
5. You don't need to ask them to be with you. They are already there.

WE DON'T ALWAYS GET WHAT WE WANT

Although it's a difficult concept to accept, the truth is we don't get things until we're ready. We have to learn and grow. We may *feel* ready *now* for that relationship, job promotion, or whatever, but we must remember that there are reasons for everything. We may have more lessons to learn, more to experience *before* we're really ready for what we've been wishing for.

Patience, patience, patience.

However, there are some things that will never come our way exactly as we'd like them. Remember the saying, "When God closes one door, He opens another." If you look back on events in your life, you'll see that although you hate to admit it, it's very true.

What we *want* may not be what will ultimately be good for us, or what the universe in its infinite wisdom believes we should have.

We must also remember to do our part to make our dreams come true.

And we must have faith.

Oh, and don't forget how many truly wonderful things have happened to us that turned out even *better* than what we originally thought we wanted!

I'm reminded of an ancient Yiddish expression that, translated into English, often sums things up: "Man plans and God laughs."

Ignoring Angelic Assistance

Angels add a great deal of joy and energy to our lives. But we're so reluctant to trust our instincts, sometimes, that we can end up making a real mess out of things, can't we?

Going on the assumption that our instincts *are* messages from the divine, we can relax and go with them. Of course, it's not always that easy, because we question ourselves, our instincts. Making decisions is a complicated business.

Shakespeare believed "to thine own self be true," and we've often heard these sentiments from our mothers, too. "Just be yourself," many a parent has preached.

But what happens when we don't trust or follow that little voice inside?

That's right, we usually end up in a jam.

With heightened awareness we always see the consequences of our actions, and when we keep track, we see that following our instincts, so long as they are healthy and harmless, is the best route to take.

You'll see that over and over again in these angel experience stories, too.

ℳY ANGEL LIST

I assign angels to everything in my life. Now, you may laugh when you read my list, but it works for me! Make a list of everything *you'd* like the angels to help *you* with. I'm always updating the list, and you'll find that you'll be doing that, too.

1. *Diet angel*—keeps me eating the right foods.
2. *Exercise angel*—encourages me when I need an angelic personal trainer.
3. *Headache angel*—has been with me for years and is probably one of my most important ones.
4. *Financial angel*—helps me to keep my finances straight, even though I'm the one who has to balance the checkbook!
5. *Business opportunity angel*—keeps his or her eyes and ears open for me, like an angelic networker.
6. *Fun and laughter angel*—makes sure I have enough of both!
7. *Safety and protection angel*—keeps me unharmed and alive and well. This one's especially helpful for klutzes.
8. *Happiness angel*—we all need one of these.
9. *TV angel*—looks for opportunities for me to share my work.

10. *Radio angel*—helps me when I talk about my work on radio programs.

11. *Book angel*—oversees sharing my work in book form.

12. *City angel*—works like a travel agent and keeps things straight for me when I travel from city to city.

13. *Home improvement angel*—helps me around the house.

14. *Healing angel*—in charge of physical, emotional, mental, and spiritual health.

15. *Medical angel*—helps me work with doctors and others in the health professions.

16. *Massage angel*—tells the massage therapist how to get the kinks out of my shoulders, neck, and back!

17. *Love and romance angel*—helps me keep love and romance alive.

18. *Memory, articulation, and conceptualization angel*—if it's in my head and needs to be communicated, this one's in charge.

19. *Travel angel*—helps with all aspects of my travels.

20. *Harmony, balance, understanding, and peace angel*—keeps me sane and happy.

21. *High-energy angel*—gives me a boost.

22. *Worry angel*—puts out those worry fires.

23. *Anxiety angel*—wipes away those thoughts that go bump in the night, or day!

24. *Fear removal angel*—helps me to be brave.

25. *Spiritual experience angel*—keeps my spiritual awareness open.

> Recently I had minor surgery on my foot, so I assigned a specific angel to help my foot heal. When I'm dealing with insurance matters, I'll assign one to smooth the way. And if I'm working on a special project, I'll ask an angel to join my efforts. You can assign an angel to anything in your life!

ANGEL PRAYERS

I ask that God's will and mine are the same.
If what I'm asking for isn't for my highest good,
then remove those desires and give me what's best for me.

Whatever I need to learn,
let me learn it and move on.

Dear angels, I pray for awareness of your presence,
and thank you for being here.
Help me to be receptive to your energies.

Dear angels, please continue to keep your love and light
shining bright throughout my life
to carry me through all situations.

Dear angels, keep me close to you,
and aware of your presence.

GUARDIAN ANGEL PRAYERS

Angel of God, my Guardian dear,
To whom His love commits me here,
Ever this day be at my side,
To light and guard, to rule and guide.

And at the end of the day, this prayer:

> *Good night, my Guardian Angel*
> *The day has sped away;*
> *Well spent or ill, its story*
> *Is written down for aye.*
> *And now, of God's kind Providence*
> *Thou image pure and bright,*
> *Watch o'er me while I'm sleeping*
> *My Angel dear, good night!*

CHILDREN'S GUARDIAN ANGEL POEM

> *Four angels to my bed,*
> *Four angels round my head.*
> *One to watch and one to pray,*
> *and two to bear my soul away.*

> —Nineteenth century

Nine years ago, Vanessa Bock was in her late twenties, the mother of a four- and a five-year-old, and driving to church on a snowy winter day when something extraordinary happened.

"The roads were icy and it had snowed that morning," she recalls, "so there was a fresh layer of snow on top of the ice. But it was a beautiful sunny day."

The young St. Peters, Missouri, mom drove slowly through the streets, worried that she might not make it to their Methodist church, that her car might careen off the road or get stuck in a snowdrift.

"God, you're going to have to send me an angel," she said aloud, asking for assistance, but hardly expecting what happened next.

"We spun on the ice and ended up stuck in the snow in

somebody's yard," Vanessa remembers. "And we sat there for just a moment. We were all okay, but I didn't know how I was going to get the car going again. Well, out of nowhere a car pulled up. I didn't see it coming and didn't hear it."

A rugged-looking young man got out of a big, dark, older-model car and tapped on her window.

"I'll help push your car out," he said, very politely.

The man had a very kind face and, wearing only a white tee shirt and baseball jacket, was hardly dressed warmly enough for that frozen afternoon. Vanessa was going to help him push the car, but he motioned that he didn't need her help. Single-handedly, the mystery man pushed her car out of the snowdrift and back onto the road.

"Thanks!" she said out of her car window.

"Then I looked in my rearview mirror and he was gone. Just like that. His car was gone, too. It happened in just a split second. I never heard his car start up, and I don't know how in the world he could've gotten into his car and driven out of there so quickly. It was impossible, but he just vanished!" she says.

Vanessa and her kids made it home just fine, but she didn't tell her husband about the experience for a long time, she says, "because I didn't think he'd believe me. But he did."

Vanessa and her husband and children are now living in St. Charles, Missouri, where she works as a secretary. Just recently, her daughter, now a teenager, asked her if she believed in angels.

"I told her the story of the man who appeared to help us in the snow," Vanessa says, "and she remembered it. Angels weren't a part of my daily awareness at that time. All I knew about them was what I'd learned as a child in Sunday school. But now I call on them all the time. I always have a feeling that someone's watching over me, something spiritual."

Remember, just as Vanessa found out, angels can intervene in a physical way. And they can provide people who will help you with mechanical problems. They seem to do that quite often. Not only will they guide someone to help you, but they will also guide *you* to find the best person to help. I've taken advantage of this angelic handyman referral service many times.

Will I Actually See an Angel in Body or Light Form?

That doesn't happen terribly often, but it *does* happen. I've seen light forms, I've seen angels in misty body forms, too. Many people have. But if you haven't and you never do, don't despair! You don't ever have to literally *see* an angel in any form. They're still assisting you.

When do people see angels? There are no rules, but most of the people who report having seen them have been in some kind of dire need, either physically or emotionally. I saw one once, hovering over my car, to protect me from an accident waiting to happen. People see them when they are ill. People see them when they are sad or grieving.

I saw one, once, in front of the bookcase in my office. I was going through a difficult emotional time, and the angel came to show me that I had not been abandoned, that I should have faith.

Children seem to be the most attuned to seeing angelic forms. Perhaps it's because no one has told them yet that they *can't*!

A thick blanket of newly fallen snow paralyzed Jill Hearn's rural community. It was late morning and her two children, Laura and James, both toddlers at the time, were keeping themselves occupied with their toys.

Suddenly, Jill felt nauseated, weak, and lightheaded. A strange sinking sensation enveloped her as she dialed the phone, trying to call for help. The emergency lines were tied up because of the snowstorm, and Jill couldn't get through. Finally she sank to the couch in agonizing pain. As she curled up she felt herself leave her body. She looked down at the Jill lying on the couch. Floating above, she felt no pain, no fear, just peace and a calm assurance that everything would be all right. The body on the couch did not move. Gazing down, she thought about her children. *Will they be okay?*

With that thought she found herself floating above their bedroom door. They had been playing inside their room, sitting on the floor with their toy blocks and cars, when Jill collapsed in the living room. *Were they still in the bedroom?*

Two giant columns of light appeared, and upon second glance Jill saw that they were angels stationed on either side of the children's bedroom door. Jill looked inside the bedroom and saw two more angels playing with her children.

"We have to go," an angel said to Jill.

Knowing that her children were safe, Jill left with the angel. Her last thought was of the beautiful mountains outside, completely covered with snow.

Jill fluttered in and out of consciousness during the next three weeks in a nearby hospital. "I found out later that five large kidney stones created a blockage that sent me into a uremic coma," she says now, ten years after that frightening yet strangely reassuring day. "My grandmother found me on the couch early that evening. She was the first one home. She had no idea how long I'd been sick, how long the children had been left unsupervised."

When Jill's grandmother entered the house she felt chills all over, as if she'd only just stepped out for a moment, and not the actual eight hours she'd been gone. It was as if time had stood still.

When she found the children in the bedroom they were exactly as she last saw them: happy, clean, and dry. "There was no evidence that they'd moved from that spot," Jill says. "They hadn't been fed, and their diapers were dry. Neither one was in need of anything."

When three-year-old Laura was asked about her day, she replied: "We played with the angels."

"I knew I didn't have to worry about my kids after that," Jill says. "I know they're in good hands, angelic hands, God's hands."

Children often easily see angels. And later they're told not to believe what they have seen. That's wrong. Jill enriched her children spiritually not only by believing them, but by teaching them about the angels' divine mission.

Barbara Theriault's angel experience, she says, was "very simple, with no bright lights or vivid colors."

Twenty years ago, she was a young mother of two, living near her in-laws. "I was pretty sick with the flu, and my husband was at work, so my in-laws came over to take care of the kids," she recalls, remembering how relieved she felt when they arrived.

"They sent me to bed, but I didn't sleep, I just rolled from side to side, over and over. I was in a lot of pain," she continues. "I don't know why, but I looked down to the foot of the bed, and even though the room was quite dark, I saw two white angels, one on each side of the bed, looking at me."

She knew that they had shown themselves to remind her that she was being cared for, not only by her family, but by God.

That was the only time Barbara has ever seen angels in form, but she knows they are always around her. "Still," she says, "I wish so much that I could *see* them again."

Retired Fort Lauderdale secretary Darline Beck says that at a point in her life when she most needed reassurance, she saw the form of an Archangel.

After a number of years living in California, Darline returned to Florida in 1989, leaving behind a life that had been shattered by divorce.

"It had been a very difficult time for me," says Darline. "I wondered if I'd made the right decision by divorcing him, but I knew that I had to get on with my life."

One night, she says, "I was alone in my bed, when I saw floating above me the Archangel Michael. His life-size wings were spread over me like a blanket, and I saw a vivid blue-white light. Then he spoke."

"Do not be afraid," the angel told Darline. "Everything will be okay."

Darline took comfort in his message, and says that whenever she gets discouraged she remembers this angelic visit and feels reassured by a sense of peace.

How Quickly Do God's Messengers Answer Us?

They answer sometimes even before you've had a chance to finish your question!

They answer right away, or tomorrow, or next week, or next month, or twenty years from now. Usually, though, we have some indication that something is going on, even if we don't have a so-called final answer. They work quickly in some areas, and slowly, step by step, in other areas. Sometimes we don't recognize an answer because we're praying for one answer and they've given us *another*! And, of course, sometimes we can't tell if we've got an answer because it takes a while to recognize the work of the angels. We're looking at little bits, and it's not until much later that we see the whole picture, and see their work.

In the early eighties, Debbie was in nursing school and living in Miami. Her friend Bonnie picked her up one evening, and the two enjoyed a "girl's night out," a welcome break from studying and hospital training.

"We had driven to South Beach," Debbie remembers, "and this was before all the major renovation they've done there in the last ten years. At the time, they were just beginning to renovate some of the old art deco hotels."

It was a warm, breezy night, and looked like an animated postcard, with the palm trees swaying, and the sounds of the surf nearby.

They parked their car on a little side street, got out, closed the doors, and then realized that they had accidentally locked the keys in the car.

"We were in a panic," Debbie recalls. "We had put our purses under the seats, so we had nothing on us, not a cent. And Bonnie had locked the door with the keys left inside."

"My father has an extra set of keys to my car," Bonnie said. "If we could just call him, he'd come meet us here with the keys. But we don't even have a quarter!"

Debbie kept saying, "If we only had a quarter to make a phone call. We could find a pay phone. If we only had a quarter."

Moments later, something caught her eye.

"I looked down," says Debbie, "and there was a bright, shiny new quarter on the ground."

They found a pay phone, called Bonnie's father, he brought the extra keys, and the two friends got home safe and sound.

"That was a night I always remember," says Debbie. "I realized I had a guardian angel. It was more than coincidence that a quarter appeared exactly when I needed it."

$\mathscr{W}$HAT FORMS DO THE ANSWERS TAKE?

The answers can be hunches, coincidences, or a feeling of "just knowing."

Or the answers can be more concrete. You've asked for something and it shows up! You've asked for a certain set of circumstances, and they happen!

And the answers may not be readily apparent because they come in parts, or gradually over time.

Ellen Dwyer, of Lauderhill, Florida, tells this story.

I have always known my guardian angel has helped me through some anxious moments throughout my life.

Each morning as I say my prayers, I include the guardian angel prayer and ask my angel to protect my grandchildren as well.

I've always referred to children and grandchildren as being "jewels in their parents' crowns" and sometimes, seeing parents exasperated with their child's behavior, I remark to them that they need to see the ruby, diamond, or whatever in the child.

I had the opportunity to go to Israel in 1992, and when at the Church of the Nativity in Bethlehem, I saw a beautiful statue of the Madonna surrounded by angels. I meditated, thanking God for my own wonderful guardian angel, and reflected that I had read somewhere that I could give my guardian angel a name. I then thought that perhaps my guardian angel already had a name of his or her own and prayed that if possible I'd learn that name someday.

One morning, some weeks later, I had been at the play-ground with my wonderful two-year-old grandson, Andrew, who had earlier at home been mischievously provoking his five-year-old brother. As I sat quietly, thanking God for this beautiful grandson, I pondered just what kind of jewel Andrew could be: a diamond, a ruby, a pearl, and then jokingly added, *coal*?

As I sat, I heard an inner whisper saying, "lapida" or "lapidus." When I got home I checked the dictionary and looked up both words, but didn't find them. I did, however, find the word *lapidary*, which means one who cuts and engraves precious stones.

I believe my angel's name was revealed to me, and now when I say my angel's prayer, I add the name Lapidus—my wonderful angel's name.

Angels work often telepathically. They give us impressions, just as they revealed the guardian angel name to Ellen. I've communicated with them in this manner all my life. In fact, they most often prefer this method because it's so quick.

• • •

What Does It Mean When We Say, "Be Careful What You Ask For, You May Get It," and How Does That Affect Us?

We've all experienced that, haven't we? The times when we want something, then after receiving it realize (immediately, in a while, or perhaps not for years) that it wasn't good for us after all.

As wise as we'd all like to believe we are, it's hard for us to know the difference sometimes between what we *want* and what we *need*. The universe will do its best to provide us with what we *need* and will be most successful at that if we're also doing our part. Now, as far as what we want, well, we can often get that, too, and with the universe's blessing, so to speak, but afterward we'll see whether it was really to our advantage or not.

Some of our lessons focus on this. We want something or someone *so much*, and the universe says, in effect, "Okay, so you think you really *need* this, well, I'll help you, and after you've got it, let's see what you learn!"

Sometimes the universe can be quite literal, as in the story I heard once about a woman who prayed and prayed for the right man to come into her life. She even made a list of every quality she was looking for in a mate. Well, she soon met him, and he was wonderful. He was everything she had imagined and more! And he was crazy about her. There was just one hitch: This twenty-nine-year-old woman had forgotten to mention in her prayers and on her list that the ideal fellow should be in her age range. When Mr. Right showed up, he was seventy years old! While she certainly liked this man, she didn't consider him a potential mate.

● ● ●

What Happens If I Ignore Their Messages?

They'll keep trying to reach you.

And if you continue to ignore them, you'll pay the price.

That price may be small or it may be great. You may learn from it immediately and then be able to act on their original message.

If they don't have much time, though, you'd be wise to follow their message as soon as you've heard it. If you're in a dangerous situation, for example, or the prospect of danger looms ahead and you're not aware of it until they make you aware of it, you'd better listen!

One of the most frustrating things that can happen is that you feel that you are being given a message, and you are not ignoring it, but you are being prevented from acting upon it.

Whether we ignore messages outright or are unable to act on them fully, there are consequences. The angels are *not* punishing us for not listening to them, so don't think of it that way. The angels are like red lights and green lights. We know what we're supposed to do when we see a red light at an intersection. If we don't stop and heed the warning, we're taking a risk.

Cassandra, now twenty-eight, was a fifteen-year-old high-school sophomore living with her mother, father, and younger brother in the Southwest when she had her most profound and frustrating experience with angelic assistance.

It was profound because she knew the guidance was true, and it was frustrating because she was powerless to put that guidance into action.

The crucial event would take place in February, but as Cassandra explains, what led up to it began eighteen months earlier.

"My mother's father died," Cassandra says. "Then seven months later, her mother died. My mother was devastated because she was very close to them. They were her security system because she and my father didn't have a good marriage. We visited my grandparents at least once a month and they came here often, too. They lived about an hour and a half away."

Cassandra's mother, who had always been in a precarious emotional state, slipped into depression after the death of her beloved parents.

"I was only fourteen, but I had to write all the thank-yous for the flowers and plants after the funeral because my mother wasn't up to it," says Cassandra, who has always had a relationship with her mother in which she is more like her mother's parent than her child. "The depression just kept getting deeper and deeper."

Cassandra's mother had to shoulder most of the responsibility for her parents' estate, and since she worked in real estate, she dealt with the sale of their home. Eight months after Cassandra's grandmother died, the house negotiations were still going on.

"My mother planned to go to my grandparents' house on a Saturday, to meet with the other realtors and finalize some paperwork concerning the sale," Cassandra remembers, the whole scenario still as vivid as the day it happened twelve years ago. "A few days prior to that I started having these visions or daydreams that my mother's car ran into a wooden pole on the side of the highway. I felt that these were prophetic visions. I just knew I was being shown something that was going to happen."

Cassandra worried about her mother driving the ninety miles to her deceased grandparents' home. She didn't want her to go alone. "My sense during these visions was that the accident was a suicide attempt," she remembers. "I knew that if she drove there alone she'd have this accident I kept seeing."

Cassandra was a hard-working student who also had a part-time job at a department store. She was scheduled to work that Saturday at 5:00 P.M., and she tried to get the evening off or switch with another employee so she could go with her mother, but she couldn't get the schedule changed and there was no one available to switch with.

"I tried to talk her into agreeing to be back home by 5:00 P.M. so I could make the drive with her and still get to work on time," she says, "but my mother wouldn't agree to that. She kept telling me that she had no idea how long the meeting would last. It was clear that she wanted to make this trip alone, and I sincerely believed it was because she was going to try to kill herself by running her tree into a pole."

Getting nowhere with her mother, Cassandra turned to her father, asking him to accompany her mother for the day. He agreed to go with her.

"Oh, don't bother, I'll be fine," Cassandra's mother told him. "It's no big deal."

Since he didn't know about Cassandra's concern—she didn't tell him about her visions—he didn't press the issue, and said okay when his wife insisted that she'd take the drive alone.

"When that didn't work," Cassandra remembers, "I decided I'd call in sick for work on Saturday so I could go with my mother. That Saturday morning I woke up and told her I was going to do that. She refused to let me go with her. She was determined to go alone."

"Mom, I'm worried about you," Cassandra said that morning.

"I'll be fine," her mother replied. "You just go to work."

What was so odd about that day, Cassandra says, was that she had planned to go out with friends after work that night, and her mother got very angry about that.

"My mom hardly ever got annoyed with me about something like that," Cassandra remembers. "It was so strange."

Cassandra wondered if her mother wanted her to be home

after work at 9:00 P.M. so the family would be together when they received word about the accident.

"My mother wasn't home from the meeting with the realtor by the time I went to work at 5:00 P.M.," says Cassandra. "And I went to work. My father went to visit some friends nearby and my brother stayed at home."

When Cassandra was told at work that there was a phone call for her, she shuddered.

"It was my brother calling to tell me that my mother had been in a car accident," she remembers. "I'd been having that vision all week, and especially that Saturday, so I wasn't surprised."

"How is she?" Cassandra asked her brother.

"They don't know yet," he replied.

Cassandra's brother called their father, and he met the ambulance at the hospital.

"Do you want to leave early?" Cassandra's boss asked.

"No," she said. "I'll be fine."

Cassandra sensed that her mother would be okay.

"It was the weirdest thing," she remembers. "I knew she wasn't dead, but I had no idea what shape she was in."

Cassandra went to the hospital when she got off work at 9:00 P.M., bringing two of her friends from work with her.

"I was so angry at my mother for doing this, and at myself, I guess, for not being able to stop it," she says. "When I got to the hospital, the police said that she should've been dead. Just as I'd seen in my mind all week, she drove her car straight into a wooden pole."

Cassandra's mother had been thrown from the car, and that is apparently what saved her life. If she'd remained in the car, the experts said, she'd have surely died, because the car flipped over, crushing the roof. No one could explain how she'd been thrown from the car, and eventually they decided that the door must have somehow flown open.

"Her injuries were relatively minor, considering what had

happened. She had two broken arms, two crushed vertebrae, and bruises," says Cassandra. "She was totally black and blue—one big bruise—and she couldn't move."

Cassandra spent the night with her mother at the hospital. Although her mother would make a complete recovery, it took two and a half years and many surgeries for her broken arms to heal.

"I never told her about my visions," Cassandra says. "People would ask my mother how the accident happened and she could never explain it. Three years after the accident, she separated from my father and went into therapy."

Although Cassandra never confronted her mother with the suicide suspicion, they had one conversation that Cassandra says was quite unusual.

"She told me that her therapist thought the accident was a suicide attempt," says Cassandra. "She would never speak about it again, but that confirmed that what I saw had been right."

Angels can easily give you prophecies. You don't have to be a biblical prophet, holy man, or wise woman to receive these accurately and exactly when you need them.

Cassandra received the prophecy of her mother's accident but was unable to stop it. When the angels couldn't stop the accident through Cassandra, they stopped it from being fatal by working directly with Cassandra's mother, tossing her from the car before it was crushed.

Miami radio producer Gary Wilson calls them "messages from the universe."

Everyone's had "something like that," he says, "a premonition, often something that can save you."

He believes that "we get those a lot more than we recognize, and we make these decisions based on these messages and it turns out okay."

Wilson, forty, says that he always has "a little voice that knows the right thing to do."

Whether he listens to it or not, "Well, that's another story," he laughs. "When I don't listen to it, I realize later that I should have. Sometimes we don't listen because we say, *Oh, it's just wishful thinking*, or *I'm being overly cautious*. We should listen more often."

$\mathscr{D}$O THE ANGELS EVER DO THINGS FOR ME WITHOUT BEING ASKED?

Of course they do!

They know what you're thinking, so they can lend a hand even before you've formulated a request. They do things based on what's *good* for you, or what will help you learn important lessons.

And, as we know, they'll rescue you, or give you the info you need in order to rescue yourself. That's when they most often come to our aid without being asked. It's their job!

In 1990, Marge Cowan, who with her husband, Irving, owned the famous Diplomat Hotel in Hollywood, Florida, walked away from a devastating car accident and fire, saved, she believes, by a guardian angel and the spirit of her late mother.

The day before, on the tenth anniversary of her mother's

death, Marge had lit a *yahrzeit* candle, which, in Jewish tradition, is lit on the anniversary of a loved one's death every year. This special candle burns for twenty-four hours, and it was very close to the twenty-fourth hour when Marge went out the next day to run errands.

She was driving alone and had taken her eyes off the road for just a moment. When she looked up again, she was headed right for a group of trees.

"I swerved left to avoid the trees," she remembers. "But I went right into them and my car flipped over."

Expecting Marge to be dead, or at least badly injured, a bystander ran to the car and pulled Marge out through the window.

"At least one hundred people gathered around, the car burst into flames, there were police cars and an ambulance," Marge remembers. "But I just walked away from the car completely unscathed. There wasn't a mark on me and I felt fine. My *sunglasses* were still on!"

When she got home awhile later, she was shocked to find that the *yahrzeit* candle was still burning—after more than *twenty-nine hours*.

"That's unheard of," Marge says. "They only last twenty-four hours. I knew it was a sign from my mother, that she had been watching over me, and that's why I was unharmed."

Looking at the candle, she remembered what a woman had said at the scene of the accident: "The angels must be watching over you."

"I knew she was right," says Marge. "And I felt that it was my mother who had been one of my guardian angels that day."

In 1969, second-generation police officer Ron Renneberg was a young beat cop working in his native Connecticut. On the force for only a couple of years, Ron already knew how valuable it was to trust his gut instincts. Every day, "something told me to do this or do that," he remembers. Listening to that "something" would often lead to arrests or information. On this particular day, following that guidance saved his life.

Ron was a few hours into the second half of a double shift that had begun at eight o'clock the previous evening. His patrol area included his parents' home, so he stopped in for a quick breakfast with his mother. His father was the police dispatcher on duty that morning and knew where his son was. Instead of reaching him by police radio, he phoned the house.

A burglar alarm had gone off at a house in a nearby neighborhood.

"No rush," his father said. "They've had a lot of false alarms at this house."

But something told Ron that this wasn't a false alarm. He ran to his police car, and sensing urgency, decided on a Code 3: lights and siren, but when you approach the house, turn off everything.

"I eyeballed the front of the house and didn't see anything that struck me funny," Ron remembers. "But something told me to go to the back of the house. I came in the back screened porch and found the door ajar and a window broken by the lock."

Ron hesitated. Normally, he'd have gone right in the opened back door of the house. But not this time. "Something told me to look into the room on the right where the door was closed. I didn't know where that door led to, but I opened it, pushing it in very slowly, and I stood aside so I could see through the crack."

It was a bathroom, and inside stood a guy Ron recognized.

"We'd busted him before for breaking and entering. He had a heroin habit."

And today, he also had a tire iron.

"I stuck the gun barrel through the door and told him to

drop the tire iron, cuffed him, frisked him, and arrested him."

Opening the right door saved Ron's life.

"If I'd opened the house door instead, I would never have seen him hiding in the bathroom and he would have caved my skull in."

Ron left the force not long after that when he was badly injured, his throat slashed "by one of the bad guys," he says now, enjoying a more peaceful life and line of work in Florida.

Where was his guardian angel on *that* day?

Ron answers quickly: "I'm *alive*, aren't I?"

Jill Hearn was awakened at four o'clock one morning by a disturbing dream.

"I knew that a friend of mine needed me to come to her," she says. "So I went to her and sure enough, she was in need of a friend."

Jill stayed for a few hours and then began the drive home. Dawn was breaking, the sky grew lighter, but Jill kept her headlights on anyway, "as a precautionary measure," as she made her way south in the far left lane of the three lanes on her side of the divided six-lane highway.

Up ahead, to her left, a pickup truck crossed the three northbound lanes and headed for the median. She was certain he'd stop at the median. She was sure he saw her approaching.

"But he didn't stop. He continued straight across, through the median and right into my lane. He never slowed down or bothered to look. When I realized he wasn't going to stop, I hit the brakes, but it was too little, too late. Finally, he realized I was there, and he hit his brakes, but it was too late."

Jill braced herself for the inevitable crash as her car continued to head for his truck.

The pickup truck slammed into her driver's door. "I watched

in amazement as the bed of the truck swung through the hood and engine of my car, his brake lights blinking just outside my windshield. I felt as though time was frozen as I watched the truck go right through my car in slow motion."

The pickup truck stopped, and Jill stared at the driver. He stared at her. "Our mouths wouldn't close. We just sat there gaping and blinking at each other."

Both of them were just fine.

"I am convinced," says Jill, "that I would have been killed had my guardian angel, Joseph, not intervened."

Jill Hearn's guardian angel, whom she calls Joseph, isn't above having a little bit of fun in the kitchen.

One day while making a pot of chicken noodle soup, she realized that there was a bit too much broth in the pot. While she debated whether to pour some out or not, she heard a voice.

"Divide the broth in half, and save it," the voice in her head suggested.

Sure, why not? she thought. And instead of pouring the extra broth down the drain, she put it in a bowl and set it aside.

She resumed her preparations, adding more seasonings to the broth simmering in the pot. After she sprinkled in dried parsley, she noticed something that clearly was *not* in the recipe: bugs, lots of them, floating in her soup. The jar of parsley had become infested in the cabinet.

Jill wasn't upset, though; she just dumped out the soup and started all over with the broth she had put aside.

"I thanked Joseph for having me set aside some of the broth," says Jill, "and asked why he didn't just tell me that the parsley was bad."

"You didn't ask," Joseph replied.

Don't think that the angels can't be bothered with little things. They love little things. Life is just a series of little things. And, as Jill found out, they can sometimes play practical jokes with the little things.

Len doesn't want his real name used, he says, because he doesn't know what his friends and colleagues will make of his experiences, and even *he's* not quite sure whether to attribute them to luck or to spiritual assistance.

He jokes that he must have had a very busy guardian angel during the spring and summer of 1993, one who kept him from death, or at least grave injury, not once but twice.

A very successful medical professional, Len is single and owns an impeccably decorated, very large home in a suburb of a major city. He hopes to marry and raise a family in this home, where he's lived for a couple of years.

He was asleep in his second-floor master bedroom when a tornado sliced through the wooded lot next to his home "and threw thirty trees into my pool." These uprooted hundred-foot trees missed the roof of his house by just a couple of feet. "Had they hit the roof," he says, "they would've all come crashing into my bedroom."

One isolated close call was enough to send shivers down Len's spine, but just a few months later he began to wonder if he was a marked man.

"I was shopping for a new car," he recalls, "and I walked into the main entrance of a car dealership showroom." Finding a salesman, Len stood just a few feet from the entrance and talked about the car he was interested in. They inched farther from the door as their conversation continued.

"All of a sudden we hear this horrible crashing sound," he says, still marveling at what happened. "The roof caved in over the entrance, exactly where I'd been standing just five minutes earlier."

Known as a no-nonsense kind of guy whose profession in the medical sciences has led him to adopt an attitude that places more importance on proof and scientific fact than on spirituality or faith, Len was at first reluctant to believe that someone or something was watching over him. But then a friend pointed out that these two close calls weren't bad luck at all.

"You're still alive, aren't you?" his friend asked. "It may have been bad luck that a tornado tossed trees into your backyard in the middle of the night, and a car dealership roof caved in, but it was divine intervention that spared you from being a victim of *both*."

Len agrees, he thinks, and wanted to share his story with you, even though he still gets that skeptical look in his eyes when he thinks about what his medical and scientific colleagues would think of him if he were to speak out loud about angels.

And yet, this is a man who believes in God and still practices the religion he was raised in, a man who intends to give his children a religious education.

Perhaps his close calls were messages from the angels: "If you believe in God, then perhaps you should remember us, too, for we are God's messengers."

We often hear that the angels play Cupid. Because Cupid, the God of Love in Roman mythology, is depicted as a chubby little boy with golden wings, he looks a lot like many artists' representations of a cherub. The cherub is an angel, but Cupid is *not*.

When the angels bring love and play matchmaker you can see the delightful evidence of their work as they leave footprints of coincidence and serendipity.

The goodness and selflessness of angels come to the minds of many when they're in love, and they often attribute these qualities to the ones they love.

"You're an angel," they'll say.

"She has the face of an angel," says a man in love.

Romance and angels go hand in hand in popular music, movies, and theater.

All three came into play recently for one couple whose friendship, courtship, and engagement were clearly assisted by the angels.

Amy Phillips had just about given up hope that she'd ever find the right man. At thirty-five, after many relationships, some that came very close to a permanent commitment, this adorable, accomplished, kind young woman threw her hands in the air, proclaiming, "I give up!"

She knew what she was looking for: a man who shared her love of the arts, especially theater; a man who was successful, bright, witty, and full of life; a man who could share his deepest feelings, his ideas and passions; a man who would be a grownup and possess all those Boy Scout qualities we all look for, like honesty, integrity, and responsibility, but who still had an enormous sense of fun; a man with a romantic soul. And it wouldn't hurt if he could also cook.

Amy had been working as an arts publicist for nearly a dozen years. She had worked in public relations at the Coconut Grove Playhouse in Miami, but had left to open her own firm just before Allen Zipper joined the Playhouse's production staff. So they didn't get to know each other until years later when they found themselves working in separate offices under the same roof.

"I probably wasn't ready to meet him years ago," Amy says. "I might have thought he was too young, and I was too busy dating flashy guys who had no substance or would break my heart. I had a lot to learn before getting to know Allen."

Allen actually does look like an angel, like a cherub with a beard.

"I know this may sound corny," Amy says, "but it's like God made him especially for *me*."

For more than a year they developed a friendship. Allen had become a theater producer, cofounding an ambitious new major theater, the Miami Skyline Theatre Company, which would perform at the historic downtown Gusman Center. Amy handled publicity for many arts organizations, including Gusman, and had her offices in their building. The more she got to know Allen, the more she was convinced she'd found a kindred spirit. He had become her best pal. They had much in common, they loved each other's company, and she had an enormous amount of respect for him. The obvious was staring her in the face, but she didn't see it yet: This was the perfect guy for her.

Allen had not only seen it, he'd been practically hit over the head with it.

He was in love.

In July 1993, while Amy was in Europe for two weeks, she thought about Allen a lot. She missed him. This, of course, confused her.

"I couldn't stop thinking about him," she remembers, "and I didn't know what to do about him. I knew how much he cared for me, but I didn't know how I felt. I was so used to thinking of him as my pal."

In past relationships, Amy was always conscious of needing

her "space." But with Allen, this never seemed to apply. She loved having him around and never gave it a second thought.

When she got back from her vacation, she called Allen immediately.

"It was a Friday night, and I'd been thinking about the movie *Sleepless in Seattle*," she remembers. "It had just come out and I wanted to see it. So I asked Allen if he wanted to go with me."

But the *Sleepless in Seattle* angel was already at work. That afternoon, Allen, thinking the same thing, had slipped a note under Amy's office door, expecting that she would see it when she came back to work on Monday morning.

"Do you want to go see *Sleepless in Seattle* with me?" he'd written, not knowing that he would speak to Amy before Monday.

"That was our first date," Amy recalls. "We'd been out plenty of times before, but this was different. I was seeing Allen in a new way, and this felt like a date."

Sunday night they saw the movie and loved it.

On Monday Allen sent Amy a dozen roses. In the movie, the characters Sam and Annie finally get together when they meet on the top of the Empire State Building. The card with Amy's roses read: "I don't know where we go from here, but I'm willing to take a chance and meet you on the top of the Empire State Building. Love, Allen."

Their romance blossomed quickly, and by October they were talking about marriage.

At the end of November they flew to New York for a long weekend to see the opening of Neil Simon's new Broadway play, *Laughter on the 23rd Floor*. Lewis Stadlen, one of Allen's partners in the Miami Skyline Theatre Company, and its artistic director, was starring in Simon's new comedy.

As soon as they got to New York, they checked into their hotel and went directly to the Empire State Building.

"I had called them from Miami to ask how late the building was open, told the woman that I was going to ask my girlfriend to marry me up there, and she told me that there was a marker, a tile in the floor of the observation deck as a tribute to the movie. It had a heart, and said 'Annie Loves Sam, *Sleepless in Seattle*, June 1993.' I couldn't believe it!" says Allen. "I didn't say anything to Amy about it."

There are four entrances to the Empire State Building's observation deck, one in each corner. Although Amy and Allen didn't plan it (the angels obviously *did*), the door they came out of was right in front of the *Sleepless in Seattle* marker.

"That was the first thing I saw when we opened the door," says Amy. "I looked down and there it was. We walked around, but it was so windy and cold that night that we kept coming back to the side with the marker. That seemed to be the warmest side of the building!"

Standing on the heart tile, Allen proposed to Amy.

"Will you marry me?" he asked, handing her a diamond engagement ring.

"Yes!" she cried out, hugging him.

When they got back to their hotel room later that evening, Allen turned the TV on, and scenes from *Sleepless in Seattle* filled the screen.

"The movie was on the hotel's pay per view," Allen laughs, "and these were the coming attractions."

The next night, Amy and Allen went to the opening of *Laughter on the 23rd Floor*, and the first person they saw in the lobby of the theater was Rosie O'Donnell, one of the stars of, you guessed it, *Sleepless in Seattle*.

Allen had been humming the music from *Sleepless in Seattle*; he'd bought the soundtrack CD soon after he and Amy saw the movie. The soundtrack was a beautiful mix of old standards and included Jimmy Durante singing "Make Someone Happy."

When they went backstage after the play to visit Lewis in his dressing room, the first thing Allen noticed was a large photo portrait of Jimmy Durante on the wall. Lewis had just put it up.

Tuesday night, Amy and Allen went dancing at the Rainbow Room at the top of Rockefeller Plaza.

Almost as soon as they arrived, the band began playing songs from *Sleepless in Seattle*. "It figures!" they both thought as they walked to the dance floor.

"We danced to 'When I Fall in Love,' " Amy remembers.

"And as we danced we could see the Empire State Building out the window," Allen laughs. "When we sat down a woman dressed as a 1940s cigarette girl came by the table with little stuffed animals. I bought a pink-and-white bear for Amy."

"Of course I named it Seattle," Amy says.

Once they were back in Miami, with their engagement weekend completed, the *Sleepless in Seattle* angel's job was over, and the coincidences stopped.

By the time you read this, Amy and Allen will probably be married. They joke that whatever honeymoon plans they make, they'll probably end up in Seattle.

Oh, yes, one more thing: Allen is a great cook.

In January 1992, Nancy's guardian angel must have gotten together with Eric's in a successful game of matchmaking.

Nancy, then thirty-nine and recently divorced, had just finished with the exhausting Christmas season at the boutique she manages on the southeast coast.

"I'd been looking forward to a quiet day at the beach," she remembers. "The weather was awful that day, very chilly and overcast, but I went anyway."

Nancy always went not only to the same beach, but to the same exact spot.

"It was my favorite spot," she remembers. "But when I got there I saw someone's towel and sneakers on *my* spot!"

So she put her beach blanket down a few feet over. She tried relaxing. Her two kids had just been home to visit for the holidays and were now back at college. The Christmas rush was over at the shop, and she could finally relax. Or at least she tried.

"I felt restless," she remembers. "It was cold, and I was sitting up, then lying down. I'd read my magazine, then put it down."

She noticed that she had company. The owner of the towel and sneakers had returned. He was a nice-looking man about her age.

"He kept looking at me," she recalls. "I'd read a bit, then look up and see him glancing at me. I'd read some more, then look up and catch his eye again. This happened at least four times. I decided that I'd say something to him next time if when I looked up he was staring again. I didn't know what to say. I thought about it and decided to just say, 'Boy, it sure is cold today.'"

Well, sure enough, when Nancy looked up again, he was looking back. But before she had a chance to open her mouth, he spoke.

"Boy, it sure is cold today," he said.

"I couldn't believe he said exactly what I'd planned to say, at just the same moment," she remembers.

She smiled at him and the two began to talk.

He asked her if she'd like to take a walk on the beach. He told her that he came south for one week each winter. His home and business were in the Midwest. Nancy met him on the first day of his one-week stay, and they had a chance to get to know each other before he flew home. They found much in common, and much coincidence not only in their present but in their past as well, including opportunities to have met before when both were at the same place at the same time.

When she did finally meet Eric, "He was on my spot at the beach, and his first words to me were exactly what I'd been planning to say to him."

The couple still conducts a long-distance relationship, with plenty of visits back and forth, in the hope that someday they'll be in the same place at the same time all year 'round.

The angels not only bring couples together but also arrange for delightful and meaningful coincidences to surround their courtship. They also protect.

Once, when in the Bahamas a number of years ago, my companion and I were enjoying a beautiful day on the beach, when suddenly I got the feeling that we were being watched. I looked around but saw no one else. Feeling a bit unsettled, I went for a walk on the beach, and while strolling at the water's edge I picked up a stick and drew angel wings in the sand, calling for protection. I returned to our towel, where he was still basking in the sun, then walked a few yards to our car to get a pair of jeans. Just as I reached the car, a menacing-looking man leaped out at me from the bushes. He wore a bandana and waved a broken bottle at me, as I prayed for help and yelled for my companion. He came running, found me terrified in front of this grubby stranger, and intervened. The two men scuffled briefly. I called for the angels to help, and as I did I saw a bright blue-white light come between the two men. With that, the stranger jumped back and stopped fighting.

"I'm sorry I ruined your vacation, lady," he said to me as he fled.

Years later, also in the Bahamas, I was learning to scuba dive. Under water I prayed for angelic help. I was not comfortable being down so deep, worrying about the current and my air and so many other things. Just as I thought that, I received an angelic message telling me that I had a choice, that I didn't have to be down there, that I could just snorkle on the surface, which was something I truly enjoyed. The angels taught me that day that we always have a choice, and that their protection is part of that.

How Do I Know If an Event Is the Result of Angelic Assistance?

Just like the feelings that we get, we just "know" that the angels have had a hand in events. The more we're aware, the more we'll learn how to recognize angelic assistance. The simple answer is that they're involved in pretty much every aspect of our lives, every moment of the day! Although that may be hard to believe, the bottom line is that we're in tune with the divine constantly. The greater our belief in and awareness of that fact, the more we'll recognize divine assistance.

Audrey's story spans three generations and forty years, bringing together two families ultimately to save the life of Audrey's infant granddaughter.

There is no doubt in Audrey's mind, she says, that all of this happened so that the child would live. "And there's no doubt that it was divine intervention that engineered it all," she concludes.

You may need to draw a family tree to follow this, Audrey warns, beginning her incredible tale of coincidence, matchmaking, and mother's milk.

In 1946, Audrey was working at a radio station in a large southeastern city when she met Sally, a coworker around the same age. The two became instant friends.

"My brother, Lou, has someone you should meet at the dance for servicemen," Sally told Audrey. "He's perfect for you."

With World War II just a few months behind them, these dances were still big social events, and Audrey had planned to go with another young man. Over and over, though, Sally kept talking about Lou's friend, a handsome fellow named Simon, who had dreams of becoming an editor and running his own newspaper.

"All I heard was Simon this and Simon that," Audrey remembers.

She went to the dance with her date and, while she was there, Sally's brother, Lou, introduced Audrey to Simon. He'd been told about her, too.

"Within a year, Simon and I were married," says Audrey.

Simon and Audrey raised three children, and both realized their professional dreams as well. Simon became the editor of a large daily newspaper in the South, and Audrey found great success as the host of her own radio interview programs.

Sally had married, too, and the two couples kept in touch frequently, although they no longer lived in the same city.

In 1968, fate brought another couple together when Audrey's college-age daughter, Ellen, introduced her friend Stephen to Sally's daughter, Michelle. This second-generation matchmaking effort worked as well as the first. Stephen and Michelle were soon married.

In 1986, Audrey's daughter, Ellen, by then married for a number of years, adopted a baby girl.

"She was allergic to all the baby formulas," recalls Audrey. "The doctor said that the only thing we hadn't tried was mother's milk. But where do you find a wet nurse in this day and age?"

Audrey related this life-threatening dilemma to her dear old friend Sally during one of their frequent phone conversations. Sally's daughter, Michelle, had a newborn, too, and she was breast-feeding.

"You know," Sally said, "it's odd, but Michelle has *so* much milk, too much for the baby to drink. She's actually been freezing some of it! What your granddaughter needs is Michelle's extra milk."

Audrey agreed. This was the answer they'd been looking for. But how to transport Michelle's milk more than one thousand miles?

"There's no such thing as coincidence," says Audrey. "The following week, Simon and I were scheduled to attend a conference in the city where Michelle lived. And since we fly our own small plane we'd be able to bring a giant cooler of Michelle's frozen mother's milk back with us. We couldn't have done that flying on a commercial jet."

When Audrey and Simon returned, their granddaughter had enough milk to last a couple of months.

"Without it she might have died," says Audrey. "I look at the chain of events through the forty years from when I met Sally to when her daughter's milk saved my granddaughter's life. It was divine intervention, I'm certain of it. First, through Sally I meet my husband. Then my daughter introduces her daughter to the man her daughter marries. Then Sally's daughter gives birth only ten days before my granddaughter was born. Michelle's body is mysteriously making all this extra milk, and we have none. We're able to transport it back here for my granddaughter. It was God's work all right."

As we see from Audrey's story, angels often band together to help when there are many things to accomplish. And you will attract more angels as the magnitude of your mission increases.

EPILOGUE

If God did not exist,

it would be necessary to invent him.

—VOLTAIRE

HAT A WORLD, WHAT A WORLD!"
sighed the Wicked Witch of the West as she melted in *The Wizard of Oz*.

Yes, indeed, what a world.

Our angels seek to protect us from the hazards of this world we inhabit, and from people like that wicked witch! As always, we must do *our* part.

In each angelic experience story in this book, angels have come through thoughts, intuition, gut feelings, coincidence, synchronicity, and serendipity. Those are the tools of the angels.

And in each story, the men, women, and children did their part as well. Sometimes that required action. Sometimes thought. Always it required faith.

To quote Shakespeare, "To thine own self be true." Follow that inner voice, that inner guidance, and it will lead you down the correct path in this world. It won't make your life perfect, because some of our lessons can be trying, but we are always where we need to be, even when we're not particularly happy about it! We will find ourselves with fewer trying times, or better able to cope with them, the *more* we listen to our inner knowing.

Our world now is in the midst of a gradual healing process that's raising our consciousness as we pray for peace and spiritual enlightenment, as science and mysticism begin to overlap, as we explore deeper into the unknown reaches of our physical and mental universes.

World leaders seek peace. Who would have thought we'd see the Berlin Wall fall in our lifetime? And then see Communism tumble down in its wake? Unthinkable! But it happened. Who would have thought we'd see Israel and the PLO come to an agreement? Just as unthinkable! But it happened.

Natural disasters have overwhelmed us around the globe. AIDS sweeps across a generation, taking away its best and brightest. Unrest and civil war mar the great freedom now enjoyed by formerly oppressed nations. Is it any wonder that we're more open to angelic assistance now than in recent decades? How many people bring the divine into their lives as the result of crisis?

It shouldn't have to take crisis to force us to acknowledge the divine, the universal forces at work in our lives.

I close with a few thoughts to live by:

- Seek God first, and everything else will follow.
- Don't try too hard; release it to the divine.
- Angels are inspiration.
- God is a power, not a man in a chair.
- Angels are beacons of light.
- Angels are great orchestrators.

Convergences

Convergences
Lionel Kearns

The Coach House Press
Toronto

Published with the assistance of
the Canada Council and
the Ontario Arts Council.

All illustrations in the public domain, or
by courtesy of Simon Fraser University
Library Special Collections or the Public
Archives of Canada; (negatives: c-6642,
c-6641, c-11201, c-34671, c-38617,
c-34672, c-34677).
Stamp reproduced by permission of the
Post-Master General of Canada.

CANADIAN CATALOGUING
IN PUBLICATION DATA

Kearns, Lionel, 1937-
 Convergences

Poems.
ISBN 0-88910-267-8

I. Title.

PS8521.E27C66 1983   c811'.54
c83-099319-3
PR9199.3.K42C66 1983

for Dorothy Kearns

They arrive. They are visible. They make themselves
present to whatever was here before their coming.
Their talking and groaning and shouting augment
the volume of sound echoing and fading here
in this place. Their energy radiates
out from this particular field of living
vegetable matter and animal protein. They take up
space. They make themselves felt. Their feet
make impressions in the dirt. They change
the scene by being part of the scene
and part of the change. They are
centres of circumstance, points of awareness
bulks moving over the ground. They are all
different and all alike. They are in this area
at this precise moment, their spirits merging
with the indigenous ghosts of the place.
Their genes move into positions on old
chromosomal chains, composing and encoding
characteristic details of following generations.
Some of them disappear soon. Some stay on
and for a time become components in a pattern
that grows more stable before it too begins
to change. It is neither good nor bad. It is
flux. It flows in waves and engulfs us all,
a process whose partial record we call history.

A continuous sense of disorder and confusion descends and threatens my life. My desk is covered with papers that I do not want to see. What will I do with them? What will I do with all this information? I want only to do my work, but how am I to begin? How will I deal with the beginning that occurred yesterday and the beginning that I completed two years ago and found again last week? How will I fit all these beginnings together? How am I to accommodate these numberless endings? What am I trying to do, and to whom I am trying to do it? Perhaps we will come to an answer or two before we are through, but I cannot guarantee it. You are free to shuffle these pages and browse, but I cannot answer your questions because I am too busy answering my own questions and posing new unanswerable questions. At this moment I know only that I am here and that others have been here before and have left something for me, as I leave something for you. Time is a ritual exchange, though the gifts move in a single direction.

They have always lived like this,
the sea in front of them, and the mountains
at their backs. And from the sides
the others, rivals, often enemies, sometimes
friends, but never to be trusted. That
is the rule, to be disregarded at one's peril
or the peril of the village. Everyone knows
the rules, but some are more proficient
in observing them. Attack only when success
is assured, and the rest of the time
attend to your public image. Be ready,
be strong, for on this coast the weak
go down fast. There are no loners here;
if individuals or small groups are encountered
they are either killed outright, or robbed
and taken as slaves. Why not? Everyone
knows the rules and everyone is a member
of a family, a clan, a community
its collective power proceeding from
the leader's reputation and prestige,
the measure of which can be taken from
the number of skulls displayed along
his longhouse rafters, from the quantity
of fish drying in racks under his roof,
from the bladders of oil stored in corners
of his longhouse, from the number of blankets

hidden away in decorated wooden blanket boxes,
from the size and condition of the longhouse
itself. Such a man becomes known
by his tools and his slaves, and the quality
of the work that he produces, and by
his women, their rank and beauty and wealth.
A leader is known for his totems and crests
and the songs that he owns and the dances
that his people can perform. His personal
value is linked to the histories
of the trading coppers in his possession,
to the number and size of the canoes
on the beach in front of the village,
to the number and fierceness of his warriors,
to his successes in battle, to the size
and splendour of his latest potlatch.
That is how he acquires standing among
his friends and enemies along this coast.
His fortune and strength rise and fall
with that of his people. There is always
the struggle, the rivalry, the rules
that are learned and followed, the life
that remains the same from one generation
to the next, a general stability, at least
until now.

Knowing what you do, doing what you
know, living in a place with people, a
people who do what they know and
know what they do: this is culture.

Captain James Cook moves his ships and men
through the empty spaces of Europe's mind.
Slowly the delicate lines replace
blank areas on the map, the margins
of human vision extend outward, the world
grows rounder and slightly smaller
as new information reaches England,
spreads to other countries
and is absorbed as knowledge.

With his new Harrison chronometer set
on Royal Greenwich Observatory time
Cook calculates his geographic positions
and navigates with an accuracy
never before attained. In Tahiti
he and his astronomers carefully
observe and record the transit of Venus
across the face of the sun. He
charts the coastlines of Australia,
New Zealand and the island complex
of the unmeasured Pacific Ocean.

The acts and hours of all Cook's men
are part of history even as they
encounter and amaze and excite
the native populations, disrupting
lives and cultures forever.

Sailing farther south than anyone
has hitherto dared, Cook has disproved
the existence of the Great Southern Continent.
Now, on his third voyage of discovery, he points
his ships northeast from the Sandwich Islands
towards the coast of America, his mission
to confirm or deny the still rumoured
North West Passage, the Straits of Anian
and the fabulous River of Kings.

Cook is commander, father, old man,
whose life and role and name all
identify and characterize this expedition
officially, then as now. Cook belongs
to his public image, to the portraits
and newspapers and history books. Even
his violent death will be a festivity,
his flesh eaten by those he most impressed.

Charles Clerke, second in command, is more
availably human because more vulnerable,
a man pressed back by implacable circumstance.
Consumptive since his incarceration for debt
prior to his departure from England,
his lungs weakened by Antarctic air,
Clerke entertains and then postpones
the idea of petitioning Cook for permission
to remain in the warm paradisaic setting
of the South Pacific Islands. He hesitates
at Tahiti because his papers are not
in order. It is the same problem at Huahein,
the same at Ulietea. At Bolabola the ships
do not anchor, Cook perhaps arranging
to avert the embarrassing encounter and
inevitable refusal of his friend's request.
At the Sandwich Islands, departure point
for the freezing northern seas, the natives
are less than hospitable, and so his dream
abandoned, the jovial, drinking, dying and
duty-bound captain of the *Discovery*
faces into the cold winds of the North Pacific,
growing weaker, more detached and weary.

They have been together on this voyage now
almost two years, each man enduring
storms, sickness, frostbite, sunburn, hunger,
thirst, bad food, fatigue, threat of shipwreck
and attack by hostile natives, besides problems
of boredom, discipline, punishment, rivalry,
jealousy and every minor irritation due to
crowding and confinement. At one point
Molesworth Phillips, Lieutenant of Marines
calls out John Williamson in a duel
but fails to dispatch him, much to the dismay
of the others. According to Midshipman Trevenen:

Our first lieutenant, Williamson, is a wretch,
feared and hated by his inferiors,
detested by his equals
and despised by his superiors,
a very devil
to whom none of our midshipmen have spoke
for above a year,
a person with whom I would not wish to be in favour
nor would receive an obligation from
was he Lord-High-Admiral of Great Britain.

Williamson, an unfortunate and unhappy man, engenders uneasiness and dislike wherever he goes. He has already killed a native of the southern islands, and treated another with utmost cruelty. He will be criticized for his behaviour during the incident that leads to Cook's death. Later it will be worse. Yet the antagonism towards Williamson is exceptional. Most members of the expedition share a close comradeship, feeling privileged to be here on this mission of peace and exploration. Other ships in the British fleet are engaged in war.

You know about life in the Royal Navy of the Eighteenth Century. You have seen those movies too, the men being lashed and keel-hauled and sent before the mast in the raging gale. Incidentally, the *Bounty* mutiny is only eleven years away, and the villainous William Bligh, whom you imagine as Charles Laughton or Trevor Howard, on this voyage is the peerless sailing master of the *Resolution*. Bligh, age twenty-four, and as yet without a commission, is reputed to be next only to Cook in navigational skill. He is perhaps not such a despicable fellow, but historical fiction has treated him badly. I wonder how it will treat me, or you.

Sticks sticking out of the sea, a disturbing sight
for Tsaxawasip and Nanaimis, two Mooachaht aristocrats
strolling along the beach south of Yuquot village.
They are talking casually and looking out to sea
for the blow-spouts of whales, Tsaxawasip
itching to rush right out on a whale hunt
to impress his colleague, but instead they witness
a strange occurrence: bare trees sticking up
from the sea. They have seen trees floating
on the water before, but these trees are vertical
and have small clouds caught in their branches.
What is happening? Perhaps a new island is appearing
in the sound. Some of the others have seen it too,
and now there is an uproar in the village. Something
very mysterious and frightening is occurring, an island
moving on the sea, an awesome and terrifying object
here now in front of their eyes. Everyone is talking,
offering a different explanation. Surely Quaots
is moving the magic island as he moves the tides
and winds. No, it is not an island but something
on the back of Haietlik the magic snake. The thing
grows larger and larger. Now Towik, a man who commands
some respect (having killed in battle more than ten men)
suggests they hide their belongings, segregate the women
and abstain from sex for ten months, but nobody responds.

No one knows which voices to listen to.
No one knows which rules apply in a case like this.
Finally Hahatsaik, a woman doctor who has a special
connection with salmon, decides that someone must
do something soon, so she takes a whale-bone rattle
in each hand, puts on her red cedar-bark apron and cap,
paints her face with red ochre, sprinkles eagle down
over her head, and goes out to meet the floating island.
Three brave young men paddle her out, with Hahatsaik
singing, dancing on the platform on the bow of the canoe,
and because she sees figures standing on it
with hooked noses and humped backs and red faces
she concludes they are *salmon-become-people,*
and addresses them in appropriate fashion, chanting

> *Hello! You Spring Salmon!*
> *Hello! You Dog Salmon!*
> *Hello! You Coho Salmon!*

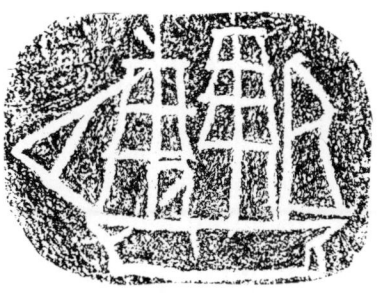

And when the others see no harm comes to Hahatsaik
some of them venture out in her wake, Wiwai
another doctor, chanting his power song, shaking
his rattles, blowing his whistle, putting the ornate
raven mask to his face, and as his canoe circles
whatever this astonishing thing may be, Wiwai witnesses
figures climbing on thick webs stretched between
branches of trees rising from the thing,
and in those webs there are round objects
that appear to be human skulls,
and Wiwai concludes these are *spiders-become-people*.
Then Nanaimus is out with his largest canoe, a crew
of forty men paddling in unison, singing his song,
and as they approach the object that is occurring there
they see figures that look like men, but men
who have fire inside their heads, for Nanaimus
can see smoke issuing from their lips, and now
Tsaxawasip, not to be outdone, goes out with his
two largest canoes, his men in their turn singing
his best song as they circle the thing, stroking
the water and beating out the song's precise rhythm
with their paddles on the sides of the canoes,
the aliens gesturing, friendly, offering them
objects made of metal, knives, this is interesting,
this is very tempting, this is perhaps
worth some grand and eloquent gesture,

and so Tsaxawasip the harpooner, a man
who will soon call himself King Maquinna,
stands up in his canoe and makes a long speech
saying that he welcomes the strangers
and if the ship will accompany him to the harbour
in front of the village his people on shore
will perform the wolf dance, and in a short time
he has given the chief of the aliens his royal
sea otter cloak and received in return a blue
gold-braided cap. This is the beginning. From
this point nothing will be exactly the same.
Supposedly it is 1774 or 1778, but these alien
figures and calculations, imposed at a later date
are totally meaningless at this moment.

And I too find myself here at the edge of the continent, an expression of genes that have drifted westward through generations. I am the newcomer encountering those others who have been here all the time or have come in the other direction. What does it mean? What is going to happen? What has been happening since we started to arrive? The evidence is there somewhere, the testimony written down or remembered and spoken, words that I search out and record and fashion again into this text which you have somehow stumbled upon, as you sometimes stumble upon a curious piece of wreckage washed up on the beach.

Now what is the matter with you? Things are bad and you are feeling a little sad? Your wife has run up the credit card accounts again this month? Your mother keeps on nagging? Your children don't understand you, in fact you realize they don't even like you. Your job is boring but what else is there? You are getting fat, and old. Yes you seem a little depressed tonight. Your life just doesn't make sense any more. Why bother? What's the use? Nobody appreciates you anyway. You are lonely again. Why not just give up? You have thought of jumping off the bridge or driving your car off a cliff, but you know you won't get around to it. Easier to do it the slow way with sclerosis of the liver or lung cancer. Strange how you never did get along with your body, or with other peoples' bodies either. So you gulp down another beer or martini and the alcohol goes straight up to the right

March 4, 1778, and on board the *Discovery*
Captain Charles Clerke retires from the quarter-deck
in a fit of coughing, while the members of his crew
rummage for extra clothing, most of it gone now,
traded in a warmer climate for the favours
of Polynesian ladies. Tonight the gentlemen
down in the gunroom are dining on rat fricassee
which they refer to as their venison feast,
and Second Lieutenant John Rickman records
in his diary that the ships
    have reached that void space in our maps
        which is marked as
        country unknown.
At last they glimpse land, but are driven off
in a violent storm that lasts more than a week.
On the 28th of March the two battered ships
sight land again, and finally put into a sound
that henceforth will be known as Nootka.

On both sides of them are high mountains
capped with snow and clothed below
with dense woods that extend almost
to the shoreline. And the land is inhabited.
More than thirty canoes come off to the ships,
which they encircle, the natives singing,
beating their pointed paddles in perfect
unison on the sides of their slender vessels,
every crewman now on deck watching the spectacle.
Edward Riou, midshipman, age 17, sees them as
   a set of the dirtiest beings ever beheld,
      their faces and hair
being a lump of red and black earth and grease
   their bodies
   covered with the skins of animals.
In the leading canoe a chief or some other
principal person is dancing on a platform
at the bow, conducting the song, shaking
rattles, blowing a whistle, covering
and uncovering his face with a carved mask
of an animal or grotesque human visage.

hemisphere of your brain and stops up
all those nattering voices and you feel a
little better for a while. The right hemisphere always gave you problems, didn't
it? God, those dreams! So much interference up there in the corpus callosum.
But we are considering Cook and his
crew as they approach the North West
Coast of America. They had other hemi-
spheres to worry about, though they
were otherwise much like you. They too
would choose more rum and less work,
and they had problems like yours until
they stepped on board those ships.

Their cultures thick as soup, the portable alphabet soup of the English, the indigenous fish and cedar soup of the Mooachahts. You claim that the ensuing events will be predictable, but you and I are merely postdicting this situation, an undertaking almost as difficult and equally as inaccurate. Nothing is certain for any of us even as we stand back to consider our experience or the experiences of these others. On every occasion the random and accidental intrude. The English hear the Mooachahts repeating *nu-tka-sshi'a, nu-tka-sshi'a,* meaning, *Come around the point into the cove.* They hear the sequence of syllables and think it is the name of this place. It is not important that they are wrong. The word and its mistaken reference go into the records and onto the charts and eventually into the minds of all of us, even the Mooachahts, who are now known as Nootkans. Mistakes and their perpetuation are the essence of evolution. But what is it that evolves here, and to what end?

DAVID SAMWELL:
Every now and then the concert would cease
and only an old woman in the same canoe
was to be heard
who made a bawling noise very much
like some of the cries of London.
After jumping for a short time
the performer
took his mask off and made
just such a noise as the old woman had done
at the same time holding his arms extended
and shaking a small box
or a wooden image of a bird
filled with pebbles
which made a rattling noise as accompaniment
to the voice. Upon the whole
it was as wild and uncouth a performance
as any we had ever seen, and that
strongly marked the barbarous and uncultivated
state of the people.

Heinrich Zimmermann, Palantinian wanderer,
has worked as beltmaker in the Rhineland,
brazier and gilder in Geneva, bellfounder
in Lyons, swordmaker in Paris, labourer
in a London sugar refinery. Curious about life
beyond civilization, he has joined the *Discovery*
as an ordinary seaman. Now two years later
he is here writing down his observations
near a cove Cook calls Friendly:

They advanced toward us
in two parties of 40 or 50 canoes
*   and paddled around the ships,*
encircling them three times. Fearing an attack
*   we loaded our guns, but at that moment*
*   they struck up a very beautiful song,*
*   beating time with their paddles.*
We were greatly astonished
*   at the exactness of their rhythm*
*   and the charm of their music*
*   in spite of their harsh voices.*
In each party there was one member
*   dressed like a harlequin*
in many coloured garments, which he changed
holding different masks before his face
*   and went through all kinds of farcical acting.*

It is the same for us, though sometimes
we neglect to acknowledge it. Sometimes
we fail to step outside the routines that
protect us. It is difficult to accommodate
the totally unfamiliar, difficult to grasp it
or speak of it or even consign it to memory. If it cannot be made more probable
it must be disregarded or rejected or
ridiculed. Happening is what is real, but
we try to grasp it by storing it as imagery
that falls into hazy sequence as we bring
it back or speak it out or write it down, so
that it forms a structure that we must call
something, so we call it time, and for
those who store these experiences in
words on paper, time becomes a line. But
do not fasten on that line. The fascina-
tion lies in the living.

Heinrich Zimmermanns

von

Wißloch in der Pfalz,

Reise um die Welt,

mit

Capitain Cook.

———————

Mannheim
bei C. F. Schwan, kuhrfürstl. Hofbuchhändler,
1781.

The sailors respond to the rituals and songs
with a sea chantey chorus or two, and a few
tunes on fife and drum. Cook judges these people
to be mild and inoffensive, but he will change
his opinion soon enough. For now, however,
he encourages them with gifts and gestures
of friendship, and finds that they show

> *great readiness to part*
>   *with anything they have*
>   *and take in exchange*
>   *whatever is offered them,*
> *but are more desirous of iron*
>   *the use of which they know*
> *and have several tools and instruments*
>   *made of it.*

RIOU:

> *By us, nothing is so well received as skins*
>   *particularly those of the sea otter*
> *the fur of which is soft and delicate.*

Thus the trade begins, the Mooachahts impressed
by the quantity of metal available on the ships
and the Englishmen glad to get exotic trinkets
to take home as souvenirs, oil for cooking,
fresh fish and food and furs to use now
against the damp and chilling weather.

Science and empire inspire this expedition.
They chart the unknown seas and coastlines,
claim in the name of the British Crown
whatever they find, and gather information.
Besides the specialists (Wm. Bayley, astronomer;
David Nelson, botanist; and John Webber, a Swiss
landscape artist), many of the officers
have academic backgrounds. William Ellis
is a Cambridge man, James King has studied
at Oxford and the Sorbonne, and the surgeon,
William Anderson, has a keen scholarly interest
in natural history and exotic languages. Yet
the ultimate impact of this encounter is economic.
A casual bartering between strangers here
will affect the politics of Europe, as it will
influence the evolution of culture on this coast,
initiating irrevocable innovation and inconsistency
in individual lives. But no one knows it yet.

The patterns persist. Moving, shifting, the repeated genotypes converge and combine in endless variety to express the unique and individual forms of the actual: persons, situations, events, institutions, cultures, states of mind. I sit on the porch listening to the sound of the creek in the evening stillness, dogs barking in the distance, and beyond that the monotonous murmur of city. As these words fall into the formal patterns of my given language, as the sentences stretch back along the page from the tip of my pen and my heart continues to circulate blood to every section and component of my body without hesitation or complaint, as I breathe the warm air that is thick with the scent of sea and warm leaves, I wonder what is happening around you as you read these words.

John Ledyard, destitute young American
searching for his distant relatives in Bristol,
has been pressed into the British Army. In danger
of being sent across the Atlantic to fight
his own rebellious countrymen, and hearing
of the impending departure of Cook's ships
on a scientific voyage exempt from war, Ledyard
has somehow sought Cook out, convinced him that
he is worthy of a place in the expedition,
and finally secured a position as corporal
in the marine detachment on board the *Resolution*.

As a boy Ledyard had run away from school
to live with the Iroquois. At college,
instead of studying law, he spent his time
building a dug-out canoe, which he paddled
one hundred forty miles down the Connecticut River
to Hartford, setting off for Europe, a crew member
of a merchant ship. After four years exile
he now regards this encounter with the coast
of America as a kind of homecoming.

LEDYARD:

I had no sooner beheld these Americans
than I set them down
for the same kind of people
that inhabit the other side of the continent.
They are rather about middle stature,
copper coloured, and of an athletic make.
They have long black hair
which they generally wear in a club
on top of the head. They fill it, when dressed
with oil, paint, and the down of birds.
They also paint their faces
with red, blue and white colours.
Their clothing generally consists of skins,
but they have two other sorts of garments.
One is made of the inner rind
of some kind of bark twisted and united together.
The other is made with the hair of their dogs
which are mostly white and of a domestic kind.
They make no use of coverings
to their feet or legs, and it was seldom
they covered their heads. When they did
it was with a kind of basket covering
made after the form of the Chinese
and Chinese-Tartar hats.

Extending outward in space and time, these wave patterns induce in my mind abbreviated images of their own condition, which I dissect and analyze, smudge and slur into general concepts, and so speak of geography, history, culture, heredity – the counters of convenient conversation and classroom drudgery, facts without feeling, abstraction so far removed from experience that I drift away quickly. I have more important things to do, more compelling material to perceive and ponder, the related images that converge at the centre of a system that occurs physically around this point as me, or from your point of view, as him. Who is he? Who are you?

LEDYARD:
Like all uncivilized men, they were hospitable.
The first boat that visited us in the cove
brought us a human arm, roasted.
I have heard it remarked
that human flesh is the most delicious
and therefore tasted a bit
and so did many of the others
without swallowing the meat or the juices,
but either my conscience or my taste
rendered it very odious to me.

WM. BAYLY:

We bought two or three human hands
which appeared lately cut off,
  as the flesh was quite raw
  and not yet reduced to horny substance.
Our surgeon also bought one
    of the human skulls.

THOMAS EDGAR:

Many think them cannibals,
yet I think we misunderstand them. For proof
  I have bought a hand from one of them,
  then desired the seller to eat it,
and offered him more iron and brass
  than would have purchased
    their most elegant dresses,
  all of which offers he treated
with great contempt
    and departed in great anger.

A series of events and images, that is all, at any time. The events take place but the series is imposed, giving up the pattern which is read and deciphered for its meaning. The world occurs in its various parts, separately; nothing is necessarily simultaneous or more connected than anything else. It is all flux, without order or meaning or purpose. That is what is given. The rest is consciousness: selection, composition, that is our business, my work for today.

The *Discovery* and the *Resolution* stay on at Nootka
for almost a month, the first extended contact
between these peoples: 193 aliens amid
four or five thousand inhabitants of the sound,
and more arriving every day as word travels out
north and south along the coast. There is much
suspicion and speculation. Do the savages
eat human flesh? Why do the strangers
have no women, or do they keep them chained
inside their floating houses? Why have they come?
What will happen next? As yet there is no
common language between them, no instrument
to hone and polish the crude points of communication.
And so they experiment, gesture, probe, learn.

WILLIAMSON:
I had no sooner seated myself than they
began to display their happy genius
in the art of pilfering.
They pretended great pleasure
in my coming down to them
and all gathering close around me.
Some admired my handkerchief,
others my hair, others my hat, whilst
some of them were employed picking my pockets
and cutting the metal buttons off my coat.
I soon caught their drift,
but thought it most prudent to dissemble.
They in return for my good nature
bestowed most liberally on me
plenty of vermin, with which they abound.

Klee hos'meet, a'ook tuh sheetl
To taste or smell, to eat, to weep

Wa'suk' sheete, ashee ack sheetl, Quao okl, wa'eeteh
To cough, to yawn, to sit down, to sleep

Ma'cook, pa'cheetle, aptsheetl,
To exchange or barter, to give, to steal

Tsook, kluts'hlaee, kluk'eezhl, seeh'sheetl
To cleave, to strike, to rise up, to kill

COOK:

We had the company of the natives all day
who now laid aside all manner of restraint,
if they ever had any,
and came on board the ships
and mixed with our people
with the greatest freedom.
And we soon found that they
were as light fingered as any people
we had before met with,
and were far more dangerous,
for with their knives
and other cutting instruments of iron
they would cut a hook from a tackle
or any other piece of iron
from a rope
the instant our backs were turned.
We lost a large hook between 20 and 30 lb. weight,
and as for our boats
they stripped them
of every article of iron
worth carrying away,
though we had always men in them to guard them
at one end of the boat
while another was stealthily
pulling her to pieces at the other.

Does language overcome this discontinuity of space and time? Can it fill the gaps of reference and consciousness? These remarkable ordinary people have come together to generate in words an occasion which is gradually taking us in. But where are you now? What time is it? What is happening, chronologically speaking? I am probably dead, or at least doing something quite apart from what is going on here between us, between you and me and these others, who are most certainly dead. Yet the words engage us all, as we perceive aspects of the same experience. You are not impressed. You scan the fine print, read one or two of my pages, focus on excerpts of Cook or Clerke or Samwell or Ledyard. What you bring to this occasion I cannot even dream of.

You think these are the actual thoughts of the men who were at Nootka in 1778? Well, you may be right, though I will give you no assurance as to the absolute accuracy and authenticity of the quotations. It does not matter much to me as long as it all fits into my poem. If Anderson or Ledyard or Burney will fill in the space it will save me the trouble. I cannot say everything. Consider, the question of dreams. If each of these persons had his or her normal four dreams on the night of April 16, 1787 then there would have been some 10,000 dreams flowing and perhaps merging on the shores of that sound. That is far too much material for us to deal with here, so let us be more restrictive. Consider the dream of Ocupah as he lies drifting in a canoe about seventy yards from the *Discovery.* Cnsider the dream of Corporal Harrison whose back is still scarred from those twenty-four lashes he ‘ received for attempting to desert in Otaheite. Consider the dreams of Weeaquat's wife as she murmurs and tosses on a cedar bark mat in her uncle's longhouse at Yuquot. Is William Ellis dreaming of Cooshicala's

JAMES TREVENEN:
An old Briton of most irascible spirit,
known for his care and vigilance,
had been fixed upon as boatkeeper.
He had been, nevertheless,
so often outwitted and of course reprimanded
for neglect of duty
that he turned as savage
as the most savage of the savages
with whom he had perpetual quarrels. At last
on an attempted theft of a metal fitting
he resolved to take full vengeance
on the offender, offering him a blow
with a thick heavy piece of wood,
but missing him it fell
with such force on the side of the canoe
as to break it
down to the water's edge.
His antagonist,
withdrawing the canoe out of reach,
was preparing to return the compliment
by transfixing him with an arrow,
having most deliberately
drawn it to the head for that purpose,

when Mr. Phillips, who had that instant
purchased a bow and arrow from another savage,
   let fly at the menacer. The arrow,
     passing close to his ear,
    diverted the savage's attention
     from the man in the boat,
and seeing the number of his enemies increase,
  he quietly laid down his arms
    and paddled off in peace.
Such hasty violence
   and fearless independent spirit
 is tempered by the phlegm
   which enters strongly
   into the disposition of these people.

wolf-face mask? Is he dreaming of heights, the nausea caused by rancid train oil in his stomach expressed as vertigo in his nightmare of falling from the ship's rigging in a storm? What is the significance, from a shamanic point of view, of Williamson's terrifying musket in the third dream of Achenoca? And where are those dreams now?

And what has this to do with poetry and eating and crying in the silence of our lonely night and making love and dying much against our wills? If these words of mine become words in your head and so connect our lives for a moment, this will be meaning. Correspondence is what we seek, shreds of similarity, understanding, compassion.

We were received and treated
with every kind of civility and attention
     by the principals of this habitation
     who made us most hospitable offers,
but our difference in taste
          and idea of what is good and palatable
would not permit us to avail ourselves
          of this part of their kindness.
          However, we were very social.
says sociable Charles Clerke, having
left behind him in the house of his hosts
a deposit of tuberculosis bacilli,
an invisible but telling memento of this
first wave of European culture on this coast.

Achatla
What is your name?

Achatla'ha
What is his name?

Akassheha
What is the name of that?

Aka chatlu ha
What is this?

A'chichil
What does he say or what does he call it?

Cook keeps his crew busy cutting wood,
replacing masts and spars, repairing rigging
and canvas, caulking the ships' hulls,
taking on fresh water, brewing his spruce beer
to fend off scurvy. George Dixon, armourer,
sets up his smithy on the deck of the *Discovery*,
hammering out fittings for the boats
to replace those that have disappeared,
finding time to forge a few chisels and knives
out of remnant metal. The work goes on
under the intense scrutiny of the natives
who commit to memory these uncommon incidents
and images, as the Europeans record their impressions
with pen and paper. These events will gradually
affect the delicate structure of men's vision,
gradually change their world. Soon these canoemen
will learn to fit wings to their own vessels,
as the British begin to realize the commercial
value of the sea otter trade. But now
during this first critical encounter
it is all spectacle, all raw information,
as both groups study each other carefully
and cautiously fall back on their old
formulas of approach and response, their own
known and trusted strategies of diplomatic
menace and manipulation.

LEDYARD:
They have a kind of armour that covers the body
from the breast downward to the knees.
This consists of moose-skin
covered externally with slips of wood
sewn to the leather transversely and made short or long
as best suits the part of the body it covers.

WILLIAMSON:
The Indians being desirous to know something
of our muskets, I endeavoured to explain its properties
and told them it would go through
their war dress, and kill them,
though at a great distance.
They laughed heartily at this intimation
and directly hung up one of their dresses
on a tree, and desired me to fire at it.
I took the musket from one of our people and
at a distance of about twenty yards
put a ball through it,
though the dress was doubled into 6 or 8 folds,
and lodged the ball in the tree.
The Indians gazed at one another for some time
with fright and silent astonishment
and it was with difficulty that I
persuaded the owner to take the dress again.

In moments of high seriousness we consider our lives in the light of our own impending deaths. It is a human experience, human as opposed to the kind of self awareness of a dog or a rat or a bacterium. The extended self-image in the context of time, that is what makes us human, but I cannot decide if it is an advantage or a disadvantage.

How to direct one's activity? How to survive in the shifting context of one's life? It is the same for you or Tsaxawasip or John Ledyard or me, though the specifics vary with our circumstance. Consider that word, *circumstance:* the circle in which we stand. But we never stand still. We respond to what is out there beyond our skins but inside the circle. The ships and the sea are the circumstance of these men's lives. This coast is the circumstance of these others. And now the two have come together to encircle and include them all, forming a context that each group must share, just as you and I seem to be sharing this text. The patterns occur out there. We perceive them and at each moment make our choices.

BAYLY:
About noon an Indian
stole a small piece of iron,
and went into his canoe with it,
and refused to give it up for some time,
which exasperated Captain Cook,
and he fired a musket full of small shot
into the canoe,
which wounded 3 or 4 men
in their backs and backsides,
which made the whole party leave us
rather apparently in an ill humour.

Meaning is always what is valuable, the meaning of the act rather than the act itself. Cook, exasperated beyond control on this occasion, orders Phillips to fire off a round of shot into the canoe of one particularly obnoxious member of the host community. What does it mean? Anger and resentment? Future respect? Fear? Regret? Revenge biding its time? Another day Cook will be more kindly. What did it mean to Cook at that moment? What did it mean to William Bayly, astronomer, who witnessed the event and recorded it in his journal? What do the star's positions have to do with the rock-salt and rusty nails festering under the skin of three persons? For Bayly the question is too obvious even for comment. What does it mean? In every case there is an important and separate answer. What does it mean to me who reads of the event in Bayly's journal and later treats it in a poem? What does it mean to you, who read my words and Bayly's quoted journal notes, at a time and place known only to yourself?

The realism and authenticity of Webber's illustrations are almost photographic. His task was to give accurate visual representation to everything the expedition encountered, and he succeeded very well. His sketches, paintings and engravings, even after they have been blurred and distorted by the processes of reproduction, give me a sense of the visual experience of the men on those ships. Webber's art was documentary. It focussed on the surface of the world he witnessed. Its perfection foreshadowed the invention of the camera. The Mooachaht's art, in contrast, presented the forms beneath the surface. It was more sophisticated in approach, more serious in intent, though the Europeans, their appreciation numbed by their judgement, found it primitive, barbarous, and crude.

The manipulation of words and images on the page is the manipulation of audience, and you know who that is. Yet this is never done without a purpose. John Webber, in turning his sketches into engravings for publication with the authorized version of the voyage, removed the conical shaped cedar hat with the little bulb on top from the head of the Nootka man and put it on the head of the Nootka woman, though he had never seen a Nootka woman wearing a hat like that. Notice the woven images of the whales and the harpooners' canoes. It is a nobleman's hat. Webber has made the change for us, so that we may be able to view both the hat and the tattooed design on the man's forehead. Such textual liberties, even when taken by me, are entirely for your edification, I assure you.

Civilisation is what they miss, what they complain of lacking. And what is civilisation to sailrs? An ideal they serve, elegance and the maintained illusion of security, the established and uncontested images of how the world is, what one knows or thinks he knows: people behaving in pleasingly predictable ways, money of course – money enough to participate in what is going on, ladies that smell like ladies, cities that smell like coal smoke and urine, newspapers, churches and church bells, shops full of goods, coffee houses, gin and ale, talk that you understand on the street, sounds that you know, unambiguous authority, the poor house, the plague. Sometimes a man is happy to leave it all, to disconnect, at first. But he looks back always and remembers. His roots are still in that other place. The alien yearns to dissolve his alienation, to eliminate the strangeness of the landscape, to transform his surroundings into the familiar. Civilization is fully knowing a situation. It is always the others who are savages. Come here my little savage.

COOK:
The women, even of the younger sort
have no pretensions to being called beauties.
Their face is rather broad and flat
with highish cheek bones and plump cheeks.
Their mouth is little and round,
the nose neither flat nor prominent,
their eyes black, little
and devoid of sparkling fire.
But in general they have not bad shape,
except for their legs,
which are crooked,
and may arise from their much sitting.
Their complexion is swarthy
but this proceeds partly
from smoke, dirt, and paint.

BAYLY:
The women appeared less in stature
than the men, and not well featured,
having high cheek bones,
and otherwise very ordinary,
which together with their being smeared over
with grease and dirt, rendered them
not very desirable objects,
but rather the reverse,
so that our seamen seemed quite easy about them,
and I never heard of any connection between them,
but even through all this nastiness
the fine rosy bloom of youth appeared
on the cheeks of some of them.
Indeed, some of the officers,
whose stomachs were less delicate,
purchased the favours of some of them,
but at a high price, to what was generally given
at any other place we had been at,
for the men seemed rather unwilling
to let them out except for something they wanted,
which they could not otherwise get,
and even this was practised
only among the lower class.
The better sort would not hear
anything of the kind.

The Englishmen's accounts of the women betray both attration and repulsion, sometimes at the same moment. Cook himself is one of the few on board never to indulge his sexual appetite, if in fact he has one, even when the opportunities have been so resplendently available in the southern islands. Less idyllic here, the axis of biological desire still spins between poles of male and female, though the barriers of custom, ceremony and attire inhibit the spontaneous urge for outright physical connection. Is taste a means of maintaining genetic uniformity within a society? These Mooachaht ladies do not taste or smell exactly like the English seamen's mothers. But the officers, at least, seem somewhat tolerant, the consequence, perhaps, of a liberal education.

CLERKE:
 The men are as often quite naked
   as in any other trim. The women
are always clothed and appear reserved.
   They are less than the men
  exceedingly dirty and very ugly.
They were offered by the men
   for dalliance to our people,
  and by some accepted,
   though this connection
was by no means general. A girl
   who was a week or ten days
   on board the ship with one of the officers
   was taken great pains with
   to be got clean as possible. This
  they could not fairly attain,
but after a score of good scrubbings
   she was a very different creature
   to what she appeared
when first taken in hand. Her colour
  was very near white as our own,
   with a somewhat reddish hue.

David Samwell writes a poem in the rigorous
metrics of Welsh verse, about the girl
he left in Liverpool, pregnant and penniless,
almost two years ago. As Surgeon's Mate
he must inspect the crew for disease
before they go ashore. Samwell staggers under
the enormity of events that include him here.
His journal shows a delicate sense of tragedy
and of comedy too. He is twenty-two years old.
When he chooses a girl he makes certain she
has been with none of his shipmates.

What is the nature of the lyric? A fine line
of the single voice alone in the valley
under the moon or facing into the wind
on a mountain cliff or raised against the
relentless surge of the surf. Is life not
song, the song once removed from the
singer? The lyric is life's complaint, the
delicate detail of passionate testimony as
human as it is irrelevant to the economic
life of the nation, and as useless as
breathing.

Do not ask me to define poetry. Do not ask me to defend my words. I live. I experience. I talk. Sometimes I penetrate the core and explore the structure of the instant with the radiant points of ecstasy. Sometimes I get down to business and write my poems. I am merely one centre of consciousness, one point around which the words swirl. But my wonder is the glimmer and glimpse of other centres, their particular circumstances, and their words.

SAMWELL:
Hitherto we had seen none
    of their young women
though we had given the men to understand
    how agreeable their company would be to us,
        and how profitable to themselves,
      in consequence of which they brought
two or three girls to the ships
    and though some of them
      had no bad faces, yet
    as they were exceedingly dirty,
      their persons at first sight
        were not very inviting; however,
our young gentlemen were not to be discouraged
    by such an obstacle as this,
        which they found was to be removed
        with soap and warm water. This they called
the Ceremony of Purification
    and were themselves the officiators at it.
      And it must be mentioned to their praise
        that they performed it
with piety and devotion, taking as much pleasure
    in cleaning a naked young woman
      from all impurities in a tub
as a young confessor would
    to absolve a beautiful virgin

who was about to sacrifice
that nature to himself. This ceremony
appeared very strange to the girls, who,
in order to render themselves
agreeable to us, had taken pains
to daub their hair and faces
well with red ochre which,
to their great astonishment, we took great pains
to wash off. Their fathers,
who generally accompanied them,
made the bargain and received the price,
which was commonly a pewter plate
well scoured for one night.
When they found this was a profitable trade
they brought more young women, who,
in compliance with our preposterous humour,
spared themselves the trouble
of laying on their paint, and us
of washing it off again. And thus,
by falling in with our ridiculous notions,
they found a means at last
to disburden our young gentry
of their kitchen furniture,
many of us, after leaving this harbour,
not being able to muster a plate
to eat our salt beef from.

You want to talk about reality. Are the words on the page real? The words in the mouths and the minds of these persons are real at the time they are spoken on spelled out. But now there is only text, or pojection from text in your imagination. Can that be real? More real, perhaps, than you, whom I will never know. Perhaps more real than I, whom you will never see.

The arrival and presence of the aliens
changes the patterns of power, upsetting previous
economic balances, intensifying rivalries,
the Mooachahts isolating and insulating
this unexpected source of wealth and prestige,
treating the two ships as they would the windfall
carcasses of whales beached by a storm.

COOK:
A party of six or eight canoes
came into the cove where they remained
looking at us for some time, and then retired
without coming alongside the ships. We supposed
that our old friends who were
more numerous about us than these new visitors
would not permit them
to have intercourse with us.
We also found that many of the principal natives
who lived near us carried on
trade with more distant tribes
in articles they had procured from us,
for we observed that they would
frequently disappear for four or five days
at a time, and then return
with fresh cargoes of skins and curiosities,
which our people were so passionately fond of
that they always came to a good market.

LEDYARD:
We purchased while here
about 1500 beaver, besides other skins,
but took none but the best,
having no thoughts at the time
of using them to any other advantage
than the purpose of clothing.
But it afterwards happened that the skins,
which did not cost the purchaser sixpence sterling,
sold in China for a hundred dollars.
Neither did we purchase a quarter part
of the beaver and other furskins we might have done
had we known of the opportunity of
disposing of them
to such an astonishing profit.

They are watching the aliens and discussing it and remembering it to tell to their grandchildren who will tell it again to their children who will pass it on to others who will speak it again to be recorded on magnetic tape, which I will play and listen to, as you will eventually hear my recorded voice or open this book and so perceive and ponder my words about them. Or the aliens themselves, the English with pens and paper writing down their notes and descriptions, which eventually find their ways to my eyes and consideration, out of which I write my poem that you are now reading, these words that have filtered through various pretexts like pebbles falling through a series of damaged sieves.

They possess it, the technology of alphabet,
that turns private thoughts and perceptions
into pieces of the world, as palpable
as footprints or scars. They bring
pen and paper, instruments to confer permanence
to the momentary act of reflection.
They come with the power to make history
and they begin to make it.

The mapmakers: Cook, Clerke, King, Bligh
and the younger ones, the student midshipmen:
Gilbert, Riou, Trevenen, Vancouver, who are
still struggling to learn the craft, compose
an intricate shoreline on paper
as others compose poems or document their
exotic experiences as accurately as possible
in notebooks and journals, most of which will be
confiscated at the end of the voyage
so the official account, when published,
will have no competition. There are exceptions,
like Rickman, who writes everything in duplicate
and will hand in only one copy, or Ellis, who will
smuggle his jottings and sketches off the ship
and sell them to a publisher for fifty guineas.
Zimmermann, too, will retain his lower deck account,
perhaps because it is written in German, perhaps
because no one believes a common seaman to be
literate enough to write a publishable work.

The occasions and events we refer to in our writing become points before and after which exist startling differences. These marks on paper, these abstracted patterns of figures and thin lines, enter into our heads to amplify and modify the existing structures that represent and interpret the half-created house we inhabit. A man consents to a universe commissioned by his community, consigned by his culture, defined by his language. Take away pen and paper, take away the ability to write and make permanent the word, use a language that has never been constrained and confined by a thousand years of literacy, and you will have a strange and different instrument for dealing with your life and situation. You will have a different world.

On this coastline two waves are beginning to converge. Two worlds are about to move together to produce the eventual ambiguous contingencies of my life. I walk the beach at evening, attentive to the sound of the sea breaking on the rocks out past the point, watching the sand-laden rivulets of seawater trickling back down the slope of the shore between each slap and rush of water. At this moment I do not know which way the sea is running. Fishing is good at the turning of the tide.

LEDYARD:
They have near a dozen different kinds of fish-hooks
all made of wood,
but was a European to see any one of them
without previous information
of their design,
he would as soon conclude they were
intended to catch men as fish.
They have a harpoon made of a mussel shell only,
and yet they have so disposed of it
as to subdue the great leviathan
and tow the unwieldy monster
to their shores. In their manners
they are bold and ferocious,
sly and reserved,
not easily provoked, but revengeful.
We saw no signs of religion among them
and if they sacrifice
it is to the God of liberty.

Do not be misled by the format of this composition. The straight or ragged right hand margin has little to do with poetry, but even my editor is confused on this point. Poetry is language focussed on its own form, yet our focus here is upon the facts as I try to include them all before it is too late. The challenge is to disguise this unpoetic material in such a way that you will approach it as poetry, a task which is almost impossible because the content of this language is more compelling than any formal flourish I can generate. Consider, for example, the idea that the Mooachaht's word for daylight is the same as their word for God.

We walked three miles in from the road to the beach at Cape Alava, and slept on the sand. The great waves of the open Pacific pounded the rocks and small off-shore islands, and the tide rushed up over the flats almost to our sleeping bags. The moon broke through the clouds and the air was so clear we could see hundreds of navigational beacons winking in their different rhythms across the Straits of Juan de Fuca as far, perhaps, as Nootka Sound. This was the land of the Makahs, the Mooachahts' cousins. They shared customs and culture, and spoke mutually intelligible dialects. We had come to this place to see the dig, where a mud slide had suddenly come down the mountain side and covered Ossette village, preserving it almost intact until now. The archeologists had been excavating it for seven years, laying bare the articles and patterns of life that owe nothing to European contact. One of the diggers, a young woman with strong arms and rosy cheeks, told us what they had turned up and what they had learned of the life in the longhouses. There were a few metal blades and cutting pieces. Some of the metal, when

LEDYARD:

We found a few copper bracelets
  and three or four rough wrought knives
    with coarse wooden hafts
among the natives of this place,
  but could not learn
  from the appearance of those articles,
or from any information they could give us,
  how they became possessed of them.

JAMES KING:

  The iron amongst them
    is of a very white kind
    and the instruments made of it
are of their own manufacture: these
  and other larger pieces of iron
    made for killing whales with
are in too many hands and too common
    to suppose the metal
    has been supplied them
  by any chance vessels putting in here
    or on the coast; the supply
must be of a more certain source,
    and of long continuance,
  although but in small quantities.

SAMWELL:
They sold us two silver spoons
 of an old fashioned make, which we judged
  to be Spanish. The Spanish we know
have been further to the Northward than this,
 and they might have touched here,
  though the Indians might have got the spoons
   and the iron by way of traffic
from other tribes to the Southward,
 as this coast is probably inhabited
all the way down from this sound to California.

analyzed, had the characteristics and consistency of Japanese iron smelted in the twelfth century.

The metal among the Mooachahts and other groups
in this area is a mystery to Cook's men. Has it
come over the mountains from Nor'west traders
or Hudson's Bay forts? From Russians
trading to the north or Spanish in the south?
Or is there a local source? At this time
there is no information, no evidence. Later
some will claim that the metal originated
with Cook's expedition itself. History
covers its tracks. As new trading metal
spreads out from these ships at Nootka
it contaminates and obliterates what was
here before, the value of the metal declining
as its availability increases.

The source of the metal and the silver spoons are not the only mysteries. Consider the odd device in Webber's drawing of the interior of the long house. You remember the story; he had to buy time by giving away everything in his pockets, then his buttons one by one, then his shoes, and finally his clothes. He sketched as fast as he could, trying to include all the details. When he was completely naked his hosts stopped pestering him, allowing him all the time he needed to finish. In the excitement, however, Webber forgot to ask about the various things he was sketching, and no one was subsequently able to identify the object in front of the carved figure beside the people seated on the bench. Even the Mooachahts, until recently, could not tell you what it was.

The Ossette site also produced fragments from a smashed wooden whale-fin 'saddle', a full-size replica of the dorsal section of a killer whale. This part of the animal was much esteemed, and traditionally awarded to the leader of the whale hunt. When finally reassembled, the sculpture displayed seven hundred inlaid sea otter teeth set out in the form of a thunderbird clutching a double-headed serpent in its talons. This whale-fin saddle, like the curious piece in Webber's drawing, was a trophy. It had a certain meaning at that time. It has a certain meaning now.

The Mooachahts still live on this coast, and the Muchalahts and the Ehatisahts and the Nuchatlahts and the Kyuquahts and the Ahts. people who perpetuate the genes and a few of the memories and customs of those we are considering here. But the land, more polluted, less productive, though in many ways the same, is no longer their land. They live only on the fringes, licking Canadian stamps for their occasional letters. What has happened? There have been no wars of conquest, no treaties; only waves of people coming and staying and occupying this space and taking control. It has been happening for two hundred years, the people coming and turning together into this, the context of my life.

COOK:

I have nowhere met with Indians
with more high notions
    of the country and the produce
    being their exclusive property.
The very wood and water we took on board
    they at first wanted us to pay for.
    but as I
    never happened to be there
the workmen took but little notice
    of their importunities,
    and at last they ceased applying,
making a merit of necessity
    and telling us afterwards
they had given us the wood and water
    out of friendship.

LEDYARD:

When a party was sent
    to procure grass for our cattle
    they would not suffer them to take
    a blade of it without payment.
Nor had we a mast or a yard
    without an acknowledgement.
    They intimated to us that the country
all around further than we could see
    was theirs.

This is a legal matter, the dubious legality of sovereignty and title. A piece of coastline, its complication of sea and tide-zone and foreshore and forest, and the abundance of its produce, is Mooachaht property. This goes without saying, though the Mooachahts say it anyway, lest there be any ambiguity. It is on record: the reasons and the testimony and the response. The claim is there in writing from these first instances of contact.

In the summer of 1933 Arthur Nicolaye, a Kyuquaht Indian, dug up a curious bronze medallion on the reserve on Village Island, some miles south of Nootka. On Sunday, January 21, 1934 the *Victoria Colonist* published the story on its front page, along with an engraving of Captain Cook and a photograph of John Webber's painting of His Majesty's Ships *Resolution* and *Discovery* riding at anchor in Friendly Cove in 1778. The medallion was one of a number struck in 1772 and distributed to various important personages on the Great Navigator's second voyage of discovery to the South Seas. There is no previous record of any of these medallions being taken on this third voyage, yet here is the evidence. I wonder what has now become of that curio, which the *Colonist* described as the most valuable historic relic of Northwestern history ever unearthed. Perhaps you know Arthur Nicolaye, or one of his descendents, and can make some inquiries.

They have converged for a brief interval
on this small section of sea and shoreline,
and now the aliens are sailing away:
one episode, one month in a four year
voyage, and highly consequential for both
the people of this coast and these sailors
who are leaving this place at last,
the ships moving towards the open sea
their great canvas sails filling with wind
while dozens of canoes follow them,
the occupants chanting farewell songs,
Tsaxawasip making his final extravagant appeal,
which is as usual eloquently uninterpretable.

JAMES BURNEY:
  As we hove up anchor
    all the canoes in the cove
assembled together and sung us a parting song,
  flourishing the saws, swords, hatchets,
    and other things they got from us.
One man was mounted on a stage of loose boards
  supported by the Indians nearest it
    and danced to the singing
    with different masks on
  at one time resembling a man
    and at others a bird or a beast.

COOK:
*These people importuned us much
to return to them again,
and by way of encouragement promised
to lay in a good stock of skins for us
and I have not the least doubt
but they will.*

KING:
*We see
many things worthy of imitation,
few of blame;
would to God they could say the same of us,
but we have left them
an incurable disorder.*

Is consciousness what we are striving to generate? Is it personal or collective? Are we in the process of generating God, who is merely a projection of the collective mind of man as it evolves? If this world were suddenly to be obliterated in a thermo-nuclear flash would God suffer an attack of permanent amnesia? What will God forget or lose when I die or when you die? Less than if we did not make these notations, did not bear witness to the experience we are having. For as long as there is something to transmit, and someone to transmit it to, and the medium of language to carry it, somehow it will continue, this experience of humanity since the beginning, spreading outward in the universe at 186,000 miles per second.

Cook sails in oblivious command to his fatal
final miscalculation at Kealakekua Bay
where he will be cooked and eaten
with Thomas, Hinks, Allen, and Fatchett
by confused and excited Sandwich Islanders.
Clerke and Anderso will have cooler deaths,
consumed by disease carried in their lungs,
their dreams of tropical convalescence
replaced by litanies of abstract words,
as the ships move through islands of ice
in the Bering Sea and the Arctic Ocean.
Old Billy Watman will die of fever in Hawaii.
John McIntosh will be struck dead in a gale
as he tries to secure the mainsail. Alex
McIntosh will die of flux in Petropavlosk
where marine drummer boy, Jim Holloway,
crippled with an infected foot, and in love
with a native Kamchatdal woman, will attempt
to desert at the Russian trading station.

I put myself inside their various individual skins. I look out through their eyes. The trees and the sun and the water are the same. It is a simple imaginative act, accomplished without much trouble, except for that reflexive kickback of consciousness, my knowledge of what is in store for each of them, their individual deaths, the absolute certainty that they are all now dead, the certainty that the *now* that has moved through each of them in turn, is moving though me, towards you. In fact, it has reached you now.

When the ships reach Macao the men will
find a fortune in furs in their chests
and on their backs. Excited by the enormous
profits in selling pelts to the Chinese,
both officers and men will petition Gore,
who has taken command of the expedition,
to return to Nootka to collect more skins.
But the standing orders do not specify
any type of commercial activity, and so
with only a few mutinous murmurs, and after
Micky Spencer and John Cave disappear
with the *Resolution*'s long boat, the ships
will set their sails for home, which is
still half a world away, the men colourful,
dressed in Chinese silks, like harlequins.

At sea more than four years, the ships
will finally put in at the Orkney port
of Stromness, to wait out a storm. There
Sergeant Sam Gibson will squander his money
and marry. But Gibson will be dead,
as will Johnny Davis, the Halifax boy,
before the ships reach the Thames estuary
and the Greenwich docks, where the men will be
immediately paid off and discharged.

Midshipman George Gilbert will sit down
to write out his recollection of the voyage,
calling it long, tedious and exhausting.
He will die of smallpox the next year.
William Ellis will sell his smuggled journal
to a publisher, and so ruin his career
in the British navy. He will die in a fall
from the rigging of a French ship in Ostend.
Zimmerman will return to his homeland and
publish his account of the voyage in German.
James King will command a 500 ship convoy
to the West Indies, catch malaria, and die
in Nice. Trevenen, serving in the Russian navy,
will be killed in action against the Swedes.
Riou will die in the Battle of the Baltic.
Webber will be elected to the Royal Academy
on the strength of his illustrations
of the voyage. Bayly will become Head Master
at the Royal Naval Academy. William Bligh
will attain the rank of Vice Admiral
and fame as the target of two mutinies.
David Nelson, in charge of the breadfruit
on the *Bounty,* will be set adrift with Bligh
by the mutineers, and die of exposure and
starvation. Williamson will be court-martialed
for cowardice during the Battle of Camperdown.

I want to tell you everything but how can
I proceed when I know so little. I want to
put an end to this text, but this series of
events has no particular ending. These
men have now reached home, a point of
divergence for each individual, each life
spinning off, twisting to accommodate its
own incongruent conditions, and meeting always an unexpected but inevitable
end. The events at Nootka are only a
brief merging of bodies at a certain coor-
dinate, to be followed by a scattering, and
other mergings and scatterings of material and personality, the segments of a
rhythm, a pulse, generating and broad-
casting waves in every direction, to interfere and merge in patterns beyond our
present focus, just as these lines will
interfere with the words and images
already in your mind, to emerge as
shapes and shadows and sounds that I
will never perceive or imagine.

Them, and me, and you – the gaps between us, the intervals. That is the elusive subject of my unrelieved preoccupation. I think of a wave moving across an ocean. I note the horizontal movement of the wave and the vertical movement of the water that accommodates it. The wave is life as it travels across time. It hits them first. It bears them up into the clamorous circumstance of consciousness, of vitality, of actuality, before it returns them to the condition that prevails after life has passed them by. The wave hits me, carrying its flotsam of testmony from them, which I use in my time before I too settle back into what you think of as the past, as the wave moves on and, by some improbable sequence of pitches and twists, its crest carries this text towards you as you rise up in your own brief and luminous moments of being. You know all this, of course. But I am thinking about those other waves that ripple through the cosmos, those that precede and follow this one that we know.

Samwell will write accounts of Cook's death and the introduction of venereal disease into the Sandwich Islands. Continuing to serve as a naval surgeon, he will also be esteemed for the verse he writes in English and Welsh. James Burney will never be as famous as his sister, Fanny, though he will become a British rear admiral, the brother-in-law of Molesworth Phillips, who will spend the rest of his life as a retired colonel, building model ships in bottles, telling tales of his adventurous days with Cok, drinking large quantities of rum, and quarrelling with his wife. Phillips will outlive everyone else on the voyage except Willy Griffin, who will live on for another sixty one years as a London cooper and then as the overseer of Watford Parish. Known as a religious man in his later years, Griffin will pass on to his son some trinkets collected on the North West Coast of America when he was just a lad on Cook's ship.

They will all remember Nootka Sound,
but only a few will return. George Dixon
will abandon his hammer, forge and anvil
to take charge of the trading vessel
Queen Charlotte, while Nathanial Portlock
will command the *King George,* both ships
dispatched to the North West Coast
to gather sea otter pelts for the lucrative
China market. Nootka will soon become
the main stopover for numerous ships
trading along this coastline. The Spanish
will establish a fort here which they will
occupy for eight years, at which point
George Vancouver, here a midshipman, will return
as British commander and diplomat, negotiating
with Don Juan Francisco de la Bodega y Quadra
a withdrawal of the Spanish garrison. Vancouver
will map this coastline, circumnavigate
the island that will bear his name, and die
at home, a hounded and unhappy man.

Their names are here around me: *Dixon Entrance, Bligh Island, the City of Vancouver, Gore Street, Chief Maquinna Primary School.* Yet the names have detached themselves from their original referents. They mean only the body of water, or the island, or the city, or the street, or the school. The names call up no ghosts. Like the old native spirits of this place, the ghosts have retreated into the gloom to be forgotten. They remain confined in old covers, locked away in vaults, absent. This absence too is culture.

Of all these individuals John Ledyard is most sympathetic, most appealing. He thought of himself as a traveller, and a friend of mankind. James Burney, his shipmate, claimed that Ledyard possessed more romantic enthusiasm than any man of his time. Thomas Jefferson said that Ledyard had too much imagination. We know now that Ledyard cribbed whole sections from Rickman's journal, which had just been published anonymously in England. Ledyard's method was something like my own. He used interesting parts of the other text and elaborated on these with his own personal testimony. Of course Ledyard had an excuse. He was being pressed by his American publisher. And besides, he wanted to finish the assignment and get on with the rest of his life. I am in a similar situation. That is why this text remains, even now, incomplete and inadequate.

John Ledyard will try for the remainder of is life to go back to Nootka Sound. Deserting the British army and returning to his newly independent homeland, he will try to organize a trading expedition to the North West Coast. Unable to interest any Boston shipowners in the venture, he will try to persuade Thomas Jefferson to sponsor an overland expedition. Impatient with the lack of response, Ledyard will decide to walk to Nootka alone, taking the long way around, hoping to be the first man ever to circumambulate the earth. Eventually he will get as far as the Siberian village of Yakutsk, where he will unexpectedly encounter his old shipmate, Joseph Billings, now in the service of Catherine the Great, who has just given orders for Ledyard to be arrested and deported as a spy. This setback will force Ledyard to alter his route. Eventually he will catch a fever and die, age thirty-eight, in Cairo, mid-point on another of his long, ambitious, strange, attempted returns to the N.W. Coast of America.

The chance arrival of these two ships
will profoundly affect the fortunes
of the Mooachahts, and their descendants.
Already they have begun to appreciate
the advantage of their newly acquired wealth,
their ability to purchase food and furs
with the currency of the metal they now possess.
And they begin to experiment with tin cups
and copper kettles and pewter basins to boil
water over a fire, instead of the old slow
way of having a slave drop hot rocks
into a basket of water. But the slaves stay busy
beating out pieces of iron and brass
into arrow-tips, knife-blades, splitting-wedges,
harpoon-heads, bracelets, arm-bands, nose-rings.
They take up their new tools to resume their work
in wood. A busy time for artisans and artists,
for there is going to be a great potlatch,
one of many celebrations to promote the fame
of Tsaxawasip, who will call himself Maquinna
becoming a most influential personality
on this coastline, though historians
will include him and confuse him with his heirs,
as Nootka Sound becomes a name in logs
of trading ships, a node on navigators' charts,
a point on maps of European diplomats.

There is still a Chief Macuenna here, near this place, among these people who, in 1978, informed the government of British Columbia that they were not interested in the Captain Cook Bicentenary, nor would they permit any of the festivities to take place on their land, their tiny patch of reservation at Friendly Cove. For them, this occasion was not a cause for celebration. The waves that washed these ships and sailors ashore had been generating a pattern of destructive interference for them during those two hundred years. And I am part of that pattern, and perhaps you are part of the pattern too.

Nothing is entirely separate, for we also participate in those events, you and I, standing or sitting and thinking of those specific individuals and actions, those particles and waves, interacting with my consciousness, as these words interact with yours, and you in your turn impinge on the quality and intensity of my experience, for my concern for you affects my care and approach to what I write. And in some similar fashion those others are constrained and influenced by our remote participation, their actions and attitudestouched and turned by my act of reiteration and your act of interpretation. Such loops are the links in a chain that binds the universe, even as it flies apart.

Other Books by Lionel Kearns:
Pointing, Listen George, By the Light of the Silvery McLune, About Time, Practicing up to Be Human, Ignoring the Bomb

Quotations and illustrations were taken from the following books:

John Rickman. *Journal of Captain Cook's Last Voyage to the Pacific Ocean, on Discovery.* London: E. Newbery, 1781.

Heinrich Zimmermann. *Reise um die Welt, mit Captain Cook.* Mannheim: C.F. Schwan, kuhrfurstl, Hofbuchhandler, 1781.

William Ellis. *An authentic Narrative of a Voyage performed by Captain Cook and Captain Clerke, in His Majesty's ships 'Resolution' and 'Discovery.'* London: G. Robinson; J. Sewell; J. Debrett, 1782.

John Ledyard. *A Journal of Captain Cook's Last Voyage to the Pacific Ocean, and in quest of a North-West Passage, between Asia and America.* Hartford: Nathaniel Patten, 1783.

James Cook and James King. *A Voyage to the Pacific Ocean.* London: G. Nicol and T. Cadell, 1784.

David Samwell. *A Narrative of the Death of Captain James Cook.* London: G.G.J. and J. Robinson, 1786.

James Burney. *A Chronological History of North-Eastern Voyages of discovery.* London: Payne and Foss, and John Murray, 1819.

James Cook, The Voyages of ... London: William Smith, 1842.

F.W. Howay, ed. *Zimmermann's Captain Cook.* Toronto, 1930.

J.C. Beaglehole, ed. *The Journals of Captain Cook on his Voyages of Discovery. III, The Voyage of the Resolution and the Discovery, 1776-1780.* Cambridge, 1967.

George Gilbert. *Journal, 11776-1780.* Typewritten transcript. Special Collections Division, University of British Columbia.

Seen through the Press
by Frank Davey
Typeset in Baskerville
Printed in Canada

For a list of other books
write for our catalogue
or call us at (416) 979-2217

THE COACH HOUSE PRESS
401 (rear) Huron Street
Toronto, Canada M5S 2G5